S0-ADW-096

Seeds of Wisdom, Slices of Life

MAGIC

Seeds of Wisdom, Slices of Life

BY

Wally Amos

AND

Stu Glauberman

BEYOND WORDS Publishing INC

Beyond Words Publishing, Inc.
4443 NE Airport Road
Hillsboro, Oregon 97124-6074
503-693-8700
1-800-284-9673

Design: Principia Graphica
Typesetting: William H. Brunson Typography Services
Proofreading: Marvin Moore

Printed in the United States of America
Distributed to the book trade by Publishers Group West

The corporate mission of Beyond Words Publishing, Inc.:
Inspire to Integrity

Library of Congress Cataloging-in-Publication Data
Amos, Wally.
Watermelon magic : seeds of wisdom, slices of life / by Wally Amos and Stu Glauberman.
p. cm.
ISBN 1-885223-47-1
1. Optimism. 2. Life-change events. 3. Success. 4. Success—Religious aspects. 5. Amos, Wally. I. Glauberman, Stu. II. Title.
BF698.35.057A46 1996
158—dc20 96-16177
CIP

Other books by Wally Amos:
The Famous Amos Story: The Face That Launched a Thousand Chips
The Power in You: Ten Secret Ingredients for Inner Strength
Man with No Name: Turn Lemons into Lemonade

To my sons, Michael, Gregory, and Shawn;
to my daughter, Sarah;
and to my adopted son, Michael Baldwin.
I love you very much and thank you
for the many happy moments
you have given me.

THE TRUE SOUTHERN WATERMELON IS A BOON APART, AND NOT TO BE MENTIONED WITH COMMONER THINGS. IT IS CHIEF OF THIS WORLD'S LUXURIES, KING BY THE GRACE OF GOD OVER ALL THE FRUITS OF THE EARTH. WHEN ONE HAS TASTED IT, HE KNOWS WHAT THE ANGELS EAT. IT WAS NOT A SOUTHERN WATERMELON THAT EVE TOOK; WE KNOW IT BECAUSE SHE REPENTED.

Mark Twain, *Pudd'nhead Wilson*

ACKNOWLEDGMENTS

I hereby acknowledge that I could not have written this book without the help of the following:

God, my creator and The Source of everything in my life.

Stu Glauberman, whose belief system and writing style meshed so perfectly with mine.

Cindy Black, Richard Cohn, and all the fantastic folks at Beyond Words Publishing. They are the nicest, most considerate, and most talented people I've ever had the pleasure of working with.

My wife, Christine, who doesn't eat much watermelon, which leaves more for me. Thanks also, Christine, for your unending love, support, and great watermelon art.

My mother-in-law, Ruth Harris, who bought me the computer on which the manuscript was typed.

My wonderful assistant, Patti Kelly, who worked long hours to get the manuscript to the publishers.

Spencer Johnson, who cared enough to drop what he was doing and help me make my book better.

Sue Zelickson, who has bestowed abundant watermelon paraphernalia upon me.

The first person who grew watermelon.

And you, dear and valued reader, without whom there would be no need to have written this book.

May all your lives be filled with truth, peace, and slices of sweet, juicy watermelon.

table of contents

foreword

This book will touch you at the very depth of your soul. Everyone needs someone to show them how to overcome their adversity—how to reframe and rethink their challenging situations in more positive, optimistic, and uplifting terms. *Watermelon Magic* will teach you how to do all this and more.

Watermelon Magic is soul talk. Wally Amos's soul is talking directly and persuasively to your soul. His magnificent spirit reminds you that you have a magnificent spirit, too. He exalts you to rise up and overcome all that attempts to conquer you and instead to conquer it yourself. Wally teaches with tremendous wisdom how to be on top of your problems, situations, and circumstances rather than letting them be on top of you.

Wally is a master storyteller. He writes in the gripping fashion of a best-selling novelist. He shares his own experiences of being caught in the quagmire of life's problems and tells how he swam to the edge to safety and success while never losing his humor, joy, and positive outlook on life. He does this with a radiant, robust smile and inspires you and teaches you to do the same.

Every "want-to-be-achiever" eventually gets confronted with problems. Wally was confronted with the monumental problems of losing the right to use his own name, losing his company, losing his finances and his bank accounts, and being beat up, at least temporarily, by the IRS. Through it all he smiled, remained happy, and knew that his soul and spirit were his and could not be conquered without his permission. He refused to give his permission to being defeated, and like the mighty phoenix, he rose from the ashes and conquered his adversities with positive thinking, positive ideas, positive action, and positive results. He teaches that you can do the same.

Wally's *Watermelon Magic* will make a positive, permanent difference in your life, your business, and your future. A book's value is not in how you feel when you read it, but more importantly, in how you can use it to handle your day-to-day situations, circumstances, and problems. Wally makes us believe that we can achieve. He fills us with the power of hope, happiness, encouragement, and the idea that "I am bigger than my biggest problem(s)."

This is a book that you will never forget. It will help you over and over again. We also predict that you'll find you want to give it as a gift to those you love so that they too will be helped.

Enjoy reading and being profoundly inspired by our dear, joyous, outrageous friend Wally Amos.

He is going to put a smile on your face, hope in your heart, and joy in your spirit.

—Jack Canfield and Mark Victor Hansen,
co-authors of the *Chicken Soup for the Soul* series

introduction

Magic is about changing and growing. It requires a belief in the process and a trust in the result. With magic there is joy and laughter.

Some people can sit down at a piano and play beautiful music. Others can only produce discord. The piano is not responsible.

It is the same with life. There is discord and there is harmony. If you regard life as a learning process, you'll achieve harmony; if you don't, you'll get discord. Life is not responsible; you are. So why not make magic?

I love joy and laughter, and I also love watermelons. Watermelons have become my metaphor for the magic of life. A watermelon starts with a single seed, and only after that seed is planted and nourished does it grow into a sweet and juicy delight.

So it is with life.

I am viewed by many as a great success. My hat and shirt are in the Smithsonian Institution. I've been in the public eye for twenty-one years. True, I've had some great successes, but I've also had my share of failures—and I've learned more from the failures than from the successes. I now count *all* of my experiences as blessings.

Watermelon Magic is about change. It's about being happy in spite of change—or maybe as a result of it. It's about growing through life's changes. You must acknowledge and accept the changes, learn the lessons, and move on. Then you can plant new seeds and create new magic.

Because I've written books about cookies and lemonade—and now watermelons—people ask me if I write cookbooks. This isn't a cookbook, but it is a recipe for a happy and enriched life. *Watermelon Magic* will help you see the wisdom of your past experiences and encourage you to plant the seeds for a magical life.

So grab a comfortable chair, cut yourself a few slices of watermelon, and read on.

Aloha,

Wally Amos

Wally Amos
aka Wallymelon

Making your own decisions

WHAT IS NECESSARY TO CHANGE A PERSON
IS TO CHANGE HIS AWARENESS OF HIMSELF.
Abraham Maslow

I KNOW HOW A PRIZED WATERMELON LOOKS WHEN IT IS SUNNING TO FAT ROTUNDITY...AND I KNOW HOW A BOY LOOKS BEHIND A YARD-LONG SLICE OF THAT MELON, AND I KNOW HOW THAT FEELS, FOR I HAVE BEEN THERE.
Mark Twain

Are you happy with who you are? Do you even know who you are? Are you living the life you choose, or are you allowing others to make choices for you? After years of living my life to please others, I can honestly say I am finally making my own choices. The result is, I am truly in love with my life and with the person I've become. Do you love yourself? I love who I am, and that includes being black. I can't imagine being any other color. I also love eating watermelon. I mention watermelon because there are those who say that if you're black and you're proud of who you are, you shouldn't be caught dead eating watermelon—or not in public, anyway. I say that it's up to me to determine what I like, what I eat, where I eat it, what I think, and what I do.

I'm well aware of the reason why black people, in most cases, advise other black people not to eat watermelon. For more than a century, white people have used the image of rural blacks enjoying watermelon by the roadside as a symbol of black inferiority.

Every culture or group—even white males, I dare say—carries stereotypes that limit people's ability to live their lives freely and fully for fear of triggering a negative response from others. In other words, we all have our own watermelon myth.

What is your watermelon myth? What stereotypes or taboos limit you? Do you protect your power of choice?

Stereotypes, racial slurs misidentified as jokes, and empty invectives masquerading as irrefutable facts are the poison arrows that racists and bigots of all colors have fired at people of other colors and cultures for centuries.

Isn't it a fact that oppressors try to claim that those they call inferior are at once dumb but cunning, slothful but powerful, weak of character but strong of will, unfeeling but overly emotional, unqualified to succeed in civilized society but a competitive threat to it? This is unspeakably absurd, and these stereotypes could only have been created by a person with a warped mind and can only dupe a person with low self-esteem.

Yet parents, teachers, and the self-appointed watermelon mythmakers have conditioned impressionable children to accept and react to other people's ideas of them. But why should anyone who knows who they are be concerned with what someone else thinks about them? How can people allow stereotypical images, foisted upon them by someone else, determine their behavior or how they will live their life?

To me, it's inconceivable. That's why I say it's OK to eat watermelon—or to break out of your own watermelon myth—no matter who you are. I will not allow the events of the past or the beliefs of others to prevent me from participating in healthy activities which bring me pleasure. What limitations would you like to move beyond?

Now, for all I know, these image-conscious watermelon mythmakers, who have allowed themselves to be conditioned to think there is something wrong with being black and liking watermelon, may actually be closet watermelon lovers. They may beg others to buy watermelon for them secretly so they can eat it in locked rooms, perhaps in closets with towels stuffed under the door to keep the flowery fragrance and slurping sounds from escaping. Or they may waste watermelon season after watermelon season wishing they could bring themselves to break this taboo. Are there pleasures that you avoid because of what people might think of you?

While others find satisfaction in working their mouths telling people what not to do, I take unbridled pleasure in filling mine with the fabulous, emerald-edged, ruby-red fruit whenever I can get it. And when I can't get it, I collect pictures and watermelon artwork and memorabilia to remind me of it. I even have watermelons painted on my pickup truck, and I carry a watermelon key chain, a gift from a friend who appreciates my love of the red stuff.

I knew that the watermelon-eating stereotype carried the heavy baggage of racial bigotry, but I wasn't sure why watermelons were singled out as a symbol. Although watermelon originated in Africa, the fruit was first cultivated in America by the Pilgrims—who we know were white. And while watermelon and foods such as fried chicken, possum, and corn pone became part of the negative stereotyping of blacks, Southern whites, ironically, ate these same foods.

Why the watermelon myth? Let's face it: When one group sets out to oppress another, they don't spend a lot of time making rational explanations for the negative stereotypes.

Not long ago, I found a picture that exploited this Negroes-in-the-watermelon-patch theme. The original print, part of a collection in the Museum of the City of New York, bears the copyright date 1882. And what's more, this work of art that mirrored American bigotry of the day was published by Currier and Ives, that highly respected purveyor of Americana.

In *The Negro in American History*, published by the *Encyclopaedia Britannica* in 1969, I found a three-quarter-page picture of a skinny black kid sitting on a wooden crate. He had half a watermelon on his lap and a humongous chunk in his hands. His eyes were wide open and his mouth was frozen in a wide smile atop the eating edge of the big slice. The picture was obviously posed and originally meant to ridicule. But in a succinct summary to the Negro stereotype in the photo, the erudite encyclopaedia editors observed that oppressors create stereotypes to ease their own minds, thinking that if the oppressed people are inferior, they don't have to worry about how they treat them.

The editors concluded: "It is tragic that whites have ever believed this nonsense; it is a greater tragedy that some Negroes have been made to believe it too."

I was raised in the Colored section of Tallahassee, Florida, not knowing much about what was beyond it. We lived in a closed society that was almost exclusively black. Naturally, I was conditioned by the closed belief system of those around me. I was a skinny little black kid, not unlike the one who was pictured happily eating watermelon. I knew all the books of the Bible, so I knew what others thought was right. I also knew, firsthand, that if I disobeyed my parents, they would make me feel the error of my ways.

I hadn't yet created the Wally Amos belief system. I wasn't motivated to make anything of myself, not to mention anything special. I had no idea what I wanted out of life, because no one ever told me what options there were. I wish someone had said, "Behind door one is this kind of success, and it's yours if only you can accomplish this task, and behind doors two and three are other kinds of success that could be yours if only. . . ." Even if I had an idea of who I was or what I wanted to be, chances are my mother, Ruby, would have dissuaded me of my thinking.

My mother was a strict disciplinarian, and my father, Wallace, usually was willing to go along with my mother—until one day my mother decided she and I would move along, and we left him.

In 1948, when I was twelve, I moved north to multiracial, multiethnic, multi-strange and wonderful New York City, and we lived with my Aunt Della, a homemaker, and Uncle Fred, a banker and numerologist of sorts. Suddenly I had junior-high-school chums who were Chinese, Puerto Rican, Jewish, Italian, Irish, and black. Comparisons were inevitable. Sadly, I found myself lacking. I was conditioned to let myself think that others were, for one reason or another, better than I was.

Back then, I had a real inferiority complex. Today we call it low self-esteem. Whatever you call it, there's no need for it if you realize who you are and what your capabilities are. There's no need to make yourself into someone else's mold. The next time you feel like eating watermelon—or breaking out of whatever watermelon myth you find yourself in—give yourself a treat. It's OK!

"COMMANDMENT NUMBER ONE OF ANY TRULY CIVILIZED SOCIETY IS THIS: LET PEOPLE BE DIFFERENT."

David Grayson

ABRAHAM LINCOLN SAID THAT HE FOUND THE IDEA OF BEING THE MASTER OF A SLAVE AS ODIOUS AS THE IDEA OF BEING A SLAVE.

"I KNEW, THOUGH I WOULD NOT FOR YEARS CONFESS IT ALOUD, THAT IN TRYING TO SHUT THE NEGRO RACE AWAY FROM US, WE HAVE SHUT OURSELVES AWAY FROM SO MANY GOOD, CREATIVE, HONEST, DEEPLY HUMAN THINGS IN LIFE."

Lillian Smith, *Killers of the Dream*

"THE WHOLE COUNTRY SEEMS TIRED OF HEARING ABOUT THE BLACK MAN'S WOES. THE WRONGS OF THE IRISH, OF THE ARMENIANS, OF THE ROMANIAN AND RUSSIAN JEWS, OF THE EXILES OF RUSSIA, AND OF EVERY OTHER OPPRESSED PEOPLE UPON THE FACE OF THE GLOBE, CAN AROUSE SYMPATHY AND FIRE THE INDIGNATION OF THE AMERICAN PUBLIC, WHILE THEY SEEM TO BE ALL BUT INDIFFERENT TO THE MURDEROUS ASSAULTS UPON THE NEGROES IN THE SOUTH."

Mary Church Terrell (1904)

"MERIT OF CHARACTER, ABILITY AND SERVICE. THOSE ARE THE TRUE TESTS OF THE VALUE OF ANY MAN OR WOMAN, WHITE OR COLOURED; THOSE WHO CAN SERVE BEST, THOSE WHO HELP MOST, THOSE WHO SACRIFICED MOST; THOSE ARE THE PEOPLE WHO WILL BE LOVED IN LIFE AND HONOURED IN DEATH, WHEN ALL QUESTIONS OF COLOUR ARE SWEPT AWAY AND WHEN IN A FREE COUNTRY FREE CITIZENS SHALL MEET ON EQUAL GROUNDS."

Annie Wood Besant (1913)

for years i always knew what i didn't want to do, where i didn't want to do it, and who i didn't want to do it with. the reality was i didn't want to be with me. it wasn't until i began to accept myself that i began to be open to being with other people. acceptance of yourself is the first step toward accepting others and leading a fulfilling life.

wally amos

Making Mistakes is Natural

EXPERIENCE IS THE NAME
EVERYONE GIVES THEIR MISTAKES.
Oscar Wilde

HALF-BAKED MANAGEMENT COST
WALLY ("FAMOUS") AMOS HIS COOKIE COMPANY;
NOW HE VOWS HE'LL BE BACK IN THE CHIPS.
People magazine, February 17, 1992

Making chocolate-chip cookies made me "Famous." Losing the company that made my name a household word made me wonder if life would ever be the same again. Despite my missteps in business, I found that my life got better and I got stronger.

Many people who know I started Famous Amos Cookies don't know I'm finished with Famous Amos. It's a long story that began in Hollywood but didn't have a Hollywood ending, and it's why I say making mistakes is natural.

I started Famous Amos Cookies in March 1975 with a little help from my friends. Others believed it was a risky business. My shop on Sunset Boulevard was the first retail store in all the world to sell nothing but chocolate-chip cookies.

Even I was amazed that a forty-year-old amateur cookie maker could achieve such swift success. The first year, I grossed $300,000. I had christened myself "Famous Amos" before I actually became famous, and out of this sweet success was born "the King of Cookies, the Father of the Gourmet Chocolate-Chip Cookie Industry, the Face That Launched a Thousand Chips."

I have always believed that chocolate-chip cookies are special and magical. Just the thought of chocolate-chip cookies evokes emotional feelings and revives happy, caring, loving, and heartfelt memories. Chocolate-chip cookies were a way of life for me before I turned them into a way to make a living. I had used my home-baked chocolate-chip cookies as my calling card in the entertainment business. A bag of free cookies always meant a warm, friendly welcome for me, although it didn't necessarily mean that my clients got the jobs.

After two years in business, Famous Amos was grossing $1 million. A *Time* magazine cover story in 1977 called me one of the "Hot New Rich." *Newsweek* called me "the Progenitor of the Upscale Cookie, the Greatest Cookie Salesman Alive." Of course, I accepted the accolades even if they went too far.

Batch followed aromatic batch. Famous Amos expanded from coast to coast. I was the nut who brought nuts to Nutley, N.J., when I opened a Famous Amos bakery there in 1976. It wasn't long before my bewhiskered brown face was to cookies what the pale-faced Quaker was to oatmeal and the Kentucky Colonel was to chicken.

I was hotter than a baking pan straight from the oven. It seemed I could do no wrong. In 1979, I made $4 million, and in 1980, $5 million. I had more than 150 people working to fill those cute little cookie bags and never-enough cookie tins with 3.5 tons of handmade, fresh-baked cookies a day. At its apex, *Time* estimated the Famous Amos empire to be a $250 million-a-year designer-cookie industry.

Within five years, my face, my trademark battered Panama hat, and my simple embroidered Indian pullover shirt had become known far and wide. In 1980, I donated the hat off my head and the shirt off my back to the Smithsonian Institution as icons of the entrepreneurial spirit that is as American as chocolate-chip cookies. Here was proof that a black high-school dropout from a broken home in Harlem could still make it in this country. For a while it seemed like a cosmic, never-ending experience. But like all sugar-induced highs, it didn't last.

In 1985, my cookie empire began to crumble. I was promoting it like crazy and having good fun, but I forgot one little thing. I forgot to put a good management team under the flying carpet. The financial side was flying without a navigator, and before long, outside investors had begun chipping away at my stake in Famous Amos Cookies.

I brought in the Bass Brothers from Texas as investors to pump more capital into the company, reducing my stake from 48 percent to 17 percent. The deal didn't last long, and another group bought out the Bass Brothers. My equity slipped again, and by that point, I was no longer involved in the day-to-day operations.

The new group was losing money and wound up selling out to Bob Baer, the founder of Telecheck, and his two sons. In 1987, the company was in the hands of its third owners in two years. I had no stake in the company by then, but I still had an employment agreement that paid me $225,000 in salary and expenses to promote the company.

In 1988, the Baers sold the company to a venture-capital group based in San Francisco. When that group sought to lessen my salary, I felt unwanted and unwelcomed. In my lectures, I advise people to move on if they do not like the people they are working with. Since that's what I was dishing out to others, it had to be good enough for me. On March 1, 1989, my contract with Famous Amos was terminated and I left the company I founded with nothing.

To secure my freedom, I signed a "divorce decree" that included a two-year noncompete clause which expired at the end of August 1991. Another agreement, which I had mistakenly thought would expire with the noncompete agreement, gave Famous Amos the rights to my name and likeness in any food-related business.

The company hadn't failed me. I failed it. The lesson was humbling. I had passed on the name "Famous Amos" to people I had no feelings for. I was no longer "Famous Amos." To me, "Famous Amos" had been more than just a name. I did not know it at the time, but I was beginning a journey that would help me discover who Wally Amos really is.

After leaving Famous Amos, I launched a career in lecturing, doing for a fee of $5,000 to $7,000 what I had been doing as a spokesman for the cookie company. I gave inspirational, motivational lectures to colleges, corporations, professional associations, and conventions. I also did some consulting. It was bread and butter, but it was never as sweet as flour and sugar and butter with chips of chocolate mixed in.

After the noncompete clause expired, I started a new company, Wally Amos Presents Chip & Cookie. I couldn't use "Famous Amos," of course, but I could use Wally Amos, because that's my name, and I thought it sounded very Walt Disneyish to say "Wally Amos Presents."

In December 1991, *People* magazine asked Hawaii correspondent Stu Glauberman to do a "Where Are They Now?" story about me. The February 1992 story described how I was embarking on Chip & Cookie, the sequel to Famous Amos, and how my freshly baked cookies and my Chip & Cookie dolls and books and T-shirts were catching on at J. C. Penney stores in Hawaii.

That story attracted a lot of attention—including some at the Famous Amos Cookie Company headquarters. In April 1992, they responded with a lawsuit.

In my book *Man with No Name,* I recount how the new owners of the Famous Amos company dragged me into U.S. District Court to try to prevent me from using my name and likeness in any business. I told myself that this was a case I couldn't possibly lose and that they couldn't possibly rob me of my name. Once again, my sense of what was right was wrong. The court ruled against me, and the upshot was that I could not use my name or the word "Famous" with the name Amos in connection with any cookie, beverage, or restaurant business. I lost the case, my name, and the Chip & Cookie venture. But I did not lose myself, my family, and my positive outlook. I learned that you don't need a name to sell cookies, you need a cookie that tastes good. So I started the Uncle Noname Cookie Company.

In March 1995, I celebrated the tenth anniversary of losing management control of the Famous Amos Cookie Company. Why celebrate these mistakes? Because I'd learned from them. I learned that mistakes usually happen for a reason. I learned that a business needs a skilled, experienced management team. I learned that I should have spent more time doing what I was good at—marketing and promoting and glad-handing—rather than trying to do all the things I wasn't good at. I also learned how vital it is to be focused and disciplined.

When I was in show business, I sat in on many recording sessions and television tapings. Whenever a performer missed a note or flubbed a line, the producer or director would chat sanely with the artist and/or the backup musicians and roll the tape again. "All right, Take 14, rolling," the producer might say. It was just a mistake. Why is it that when someone makes a mistake in business or in personal relationships, it's cause for anger? Humans aren't perfect—even if they're singing stars, movie stars, or cookie bakers. We all make mistakes. We're all in a state of training, a state of becoming—becoming a better worker, a better student, a better parent, a better spouse, a better friend, or a better person.

I remember the time I caught a worker who had burned a rack with twenty trays of cookies. I was about to chew the worker out when an inner voice reminded me of all the times I had burned cookies. I settled down and explained to the worker the cost involved in sacrificing twenty trays of cookies on the altar of carelessness. I told the worker to do another take—more carefully. Patience and understanding and sound advice can go a long way in guiding and encouraging employees and friends through their mistakes.

Another thing I've learned from my mistakes is that it's important to work from your strengths. Don't spread yourself too thin. Focus your time and energy on the things you do best. Leave the rest to the other members of the team.

When all is said and done, mistakes are the process through which we in turn create success. Mistakes create the foundation for our life. That foundation is experience, which in turn creates the light that leads us into our future. That light is called wisdom.

SEEDS OF WISDOM
SLICES OF LIFE

THE REAL VOYAGE OF DISCOVERY CONSISTS NOT IN EXPLORING NEW LANDSCAPES BUT IN HAVING NEW EYES. MISTAKES HELP YOU TO EXPAND YOUR HORIZONS.

"I AM UPSET, NOT BY EVENTS, BUT RATHER BY THE WAY I VIEW THEM."
Epictetus (first century A.D.)

LOOKING AT MISTAKES AS LEARNING EXPERIENCES AND STEPPING-STONES HELPS YOU TO SEE THAT FAILURE IS SOMEONE ELSE'S OPINION OF THE OUTCOME OF A SITUATION.

"FAILURE IS ONLY THE OPPORTUNITY TO BEGIN AGAIN . . . MORE INTELLIGENTLY."
Henry Ford

It took Thomas Edison 10,000 attempts before he discovered the carbon filament for the light bulb. He did not view each effort as a mistake or a failure; rather, he saw each effort advancing him closer to success. He had 9,999 mistakes before success. Each time he reviewed the previous take and started again knowing more about what would work and what would not. How many takes do you try before giving up? The only way you can fail is by giving up.

The dictionary defines mistake as "error, to understand wrongly, misinterpret," which means that mistakes can be changed; they need not be fatal.

"Every great mistake has a halfway moment, a split second when it can be recalled and perhaps remedied. We're all in training, practicing."

Pearl S. Buck

Mistakes are natural.
Mistakes are how we learn.
When we stop making mistakes,
we stop learning and growing.
But repeating the same mistake
over and over is not continuous
learning—it's not paying
attention.

Wally Amos

Accepting your past

I TELL YOU THE PAST IS A BUCKET OF ASHES.
Carl Sandburg

**THE PAST IS A FOREIGN COUNTRY.
THEY DO THINGS DIFFERENTLY THERE.**
L. P. Hartley

What aspects of your past are still unresolved? What lurks in the shadows of your past that frightens you? We all have a past. Without our past we would have no present and no future. Who you are today is directly related to your past. You can't run from it. You can't hide from it. The only thing you can do to make it leave you alone is to accept it.

What's the worst thing you've ever done? Have you told a lie that cost a friend dearly or hurt someone you loved? Whoever you are today, you are that person as a direct result of the things you've done—and failed to do—plus all the decisions you've made and the way you've handled every situation. You are also the product of all the things people have done to you.

It's human nature to pat yourself on the back and sing your praises for all the good things you did that turned out the way you and everyone around you wanted them to turn out. For most of us, however, there are fewer of those feel-good experiences than the challenging experiences or the feel-bad experiences. Personally, my growth has come more from my challenges and failures than from my feel-good experiences. Challenging experiences can be your own personal growth chamber. They're a great opportunity given to you by your past. Eventually, you have to recognize and accept your past as the only foundation that you have to build your future on, and then you have to start building.

Learning in the school of experience isn't like learning in regular school. In the school of experience, you take the test first and *then* you review what you've learned. Your past can be a great teacher, if you are prepared to pay the tuition. But sometimes you think you're paid up only to learn that you've got to pay and pay. In this regard, the school of experience is a lot like regular school: If you don't get the lesson, you repeat the experience again and again.

If you were to write my life story, you would probably conclude that losing the Famous Amos Cookie Company was one of the worst things that ever happened to me. That was seven years ago, and I haven't had a regular job or paycheck since. In financial terms, the only things I've done with regularity are amass debt and miss payments. As my biographer, looking at the spreadsheet of my financial life, you would probably conclude that I was living a life of desperation. Some days my bank account, my accountant, and my wife would agree with you.

In fact, living in the wake of losing Famous Amos has been a very positive experience for me, even though you may not see it on paper. That's because all of my growth has been in the only place where it really counts, and that's inner growth. I've learned that I was not a house (which the bank auctioned off and I regained with the help of a friend), a company, or a name. I've learned to live by my wits, hand-to-mouth, month-to-month, finding solutions in the nick of time without ever wondering where they would come from. I have confirmed for myself that there is truly a Higher Power in the Universe than myself and that this Power will support me and sustain me moment-to-moment and day-to-day. I am much stronger now because I have the wisdom of my experience. It is what Marilyn Ferguson referred to in her book *The Aquarian Experience* as "direct knowing." This has been and continues to be an exhilarating journey. To enjoy the challenges that confront us each day, we have to confront the past that we can't erase.

We begin life as the product of our environment. Where we grow from there is up to us. From our first cry at birth, we are blatantly and subliminally programmed by others. Most of our earliest programming comes from our parents. Whether we like it or realize it, we absorb their habits and beliefs at an age when we are under their control and unable to do much about it. Their concerns and values act on us for the better part of our lives, and unless we redefine ourselves and form our own beliefs, we continue to run our parents' programs in our thoughts and actions. When we have an experience that's not to our liking, we take it personally, as if the misfortune is a part of us.

Many people have trouble separating what they do and what happens to them from who they are. They think they are their behavior. You are not your behavior. You are separate from and more than your behavior. Who you are is much more important than how you behave. When you begin to appreciate the fantastic being that you are, you will also begin to see a change in your behavior. Coming to terms with our past helps us to love ourselves, which changes how we relate to others in our world.

When something unexpected happens, we have to look at it as Bette Midler looked at human enmity: "From a distance." Looking at life's situations from a distance is the first step toward finding a solution and preventing them from happening again. By separating yourself from your experiences, you are able to move on with your life. If you don't, you're stuck in the puddle of the past without a paddle.

The Wally Amos view is that most of us march into adulthood having been imprinted by everyone around us. We let people tell us how to dress. They drum into us the names of the designer-label clothing that we need to wear to the point where our personal taste in clothing does not seem to matter. They influence the choice of soap we use, the car we drive, the place we live, and all the things we ought to buy for our house. The list goes on and on until we begin to blame whoever it is we call "they" for everything we decide and everything that happens to us.

I once received a letter from a man whose wife had lost her job. She became bitter and afraid to experience anything new. She undermined her own efforts and put all the blame on others—all the "theys" and "thems" who stood in her way. Who are "they"? By what authority do "they" control us? By our authority! Eleanor Roosevelt was right when she said, "No one can make you feel inferior without your permission." Too often we are conditioned by others, and we give them permission to control us.

A friend, raised in Australia, told me he was fifty-five years old by the time he realized he had inherited his father's insensitive, domineering personality. Only after becoming aware of it was he able to look inside himself to discover his own personality and belief system.

Another friend recalled that he had undergone so many abdominal operations as a toddler that he was not expected to live. His mother often warned relatives to be careful with him because he was sick and wasn't going to live long. Not only did Charles live, but he lived to be a daredevil, always on the edge, constantly challenging his mortality, testing his mother's thesis that he wasn't going to live long anyway. He had many close calls. Only now that he is close to sixty years old is he becoming more introspective and seeking answers within.

For many years I wrestled with my father's characteristics. My father had no respect for my mother, and he often cheated on her. I went through many failed relationships and two failed marriages before realizing that I lacked respect for and commitment to the women in my life, much as my father had. I finally realized why my relationships hadn't worked. I had failed to make a commitment to them. It was part of my conditioning. It's what I knew from my past. It was a pattern that I brought into my relationship with my current wife, Christine.

During the early days of our relationship, I told her, "Look, I've failed as a husband twice before. We can live together, because I can be a good boyfriend, but we can't get married because I am not a good husband."

That's the kind of conditioning you can't get from a shampoo bottle. Becoming aware of your actions is the first step toward changing how you behave. First I made the decision to change. Understanding that I had not made a commitment in the past, I told myself I was going to make a commitment this time. I recognized that in past relationships I was always ready to cite the smallest thing as a good reason to leave the relationship.

This time, I decided it was going to be different. I was going to get involved in the relationship and stay involved. I did some backsliding because my imprinting was so deep. However, I have used those times to take a closer look at those old patterns and to see that they were not really mine but my father's, and so my behavior has become much more responsible. Confronting my past and putting it to good use helped me build a stronger foundation.

If you are committed to a relationship, you must stick with it through thick and thin. Instead of looking for ways to get out, look for ways to work it out. When you are involved in a relationship, a career, or a task, you shouldn't look for reasons to fail, even if you failed in the past. You must look for reasons to succeed, because you have a purpose. You can begin by transforming your belief system. It will become the beacon that can help you escape from the prison of the past. The secret to success in anything is to keep your mind on the things you want and off the things you don't want.

I recently became aware of past conditioning that might have held me back financially. After a lecture, a gentleman approached me and offered to pay me $1,000 to meet with him and a friend for one hour. He thought his friend would benefit from meeting and talking with me. My first reaction was that my time was not worth that much money. I had no degree and no professional training in helping people through their challenges, but that's exactly what I had done many times through my lectures, interviews, books, tapes, and in one-on-one meetings. My past imprints of unworthiness were so strong they jumped in front of the truth. I resolved the issue by suggesting we meet the next morning without any financial commitment. I told the generous gentleman that if he and his friend felt they had received benefit from our being together, he could pay me whatever he felt it was worth.

We met the next morning and had a very meaningful one-and-a-half-hour session together. When the meeting had concluded, the gentleman handed me an envelope with $250 cash and a blank, signed check. He told me I could fill in the balance. Now the ball was back in my court. I still had to decide how much I thought my time was worth. My initial thought was to fill in the balance for $750 and treat $500 as a loan. I was still feeling unworthy. Then it occurred to me that I was denying someone else the opportunity to give and also that I thought less of myself than did the person giving me the money. It also occurred to me that God had sent this wonderful angel with a much-needed cash gift, and I was still refusing it. I was finally able to overpower past conditioning and accept the full $1,000 for services I had rendered. That experience has done much to elevate my self-esteem. There is a phrase from *A Course in Miracles* which sums it up: "To believe in your littleness is arrogant because it means you think your evaluation of yourself is truer than God's."

More and more I am beginning to see the past as something that needs to be opened up and written upon. It's as if we have been given a template. It is up to us to use that template. If you can't create something with it, you're condemned to relive the past, making the same mistakes in personal or business relationships that you've already made. If you continue to make the same mistakes, you can expect to get the same results.

The first time a business or a relationship fails, you say to yourself, "I'm not ever going to do that again." You say that because you did something and it failed. You have to look at *why* you failed. Somewhere in that failure, there are important lessons to be learned so that the next time a business opportunity or a romantic opportunity presents it or his or herself, you will know what not to do. You have to do something new or something different. You can't keep planting papaya seeds if you want watermelons. Sooner or later, you will have to plant watermelon seeds to harvest watermelons.

They say hindsight is always 100 percent. That's why we laugh when we read about myopic visionaries of the past: Western Union said in 1876 that the telephone was a useless invention. Britain's Lord Kelvin said in 1895 that machines would never fly. Advisors told David Sarnoff in the 1920s that his wireless music box, the radio, would have no commercial application because no one would pay for a message sent to no one in particular. A few years later, one of the silent-movie-making Warner Brothers asked, "Who the hell wants to hear actors talk?" Thomas Watson, the chairman of International Business Machines in 1943, didn't think there was much of a market for a new invention called the computer. Twenty-five years later, IBM's Advance Computer Systems Division didn't see any market for the microchip. When Steven Jobs and Steve Wozniak tried to interest Atari and Hewlett-Packard in their invention, the personal computer, they were disappointed to the core. They had to go out and form their own company, Apple.

There is always someone to tell you that something can't be done. These people are allowing their negative, nonproductive past to constantly reproduce their future. If inventors and other visionaries had spent all their time listening to naysayers, things that had never been done before would never have gotten done! Or as they say, "The person who says it cannot be done is usually watching someone do it."

When I started the Famous Amos Cookie Company, people told me I couldn't start a business that sold only chocolate-chip cookies. The reason they said I couldn't do it was because it had never been done before. I told them, "It's time somebody did, and that somebody is going to be me." They made me more determined than ever to do it.

I believe that if you weren't meant to do something, you wouldn't have gotten the idea, because everything happens as a result of ideas. I could have believed just as easily that my past creates my future, saying that because it hadn't been done, I would not be able to do it. However, I chose to believe that because I had the idea to start a company selling only chocolate-chip cookies, this meant it was time for it to happen.

In my years of encounters with "bad" experiences, I've learned that nothing is ever as bad as it first might seem. I don't care how bad you think it is, it's always better than that. People say that when you hit bottom, there's no place to look but up. The poet and author Richard Farina said that he had been down so long it looked like up to him. I say that when you think you've hit bottom, it pays to look up with a 360-degree turn, because if you do, you're bound to see something you've not seen before, something you can grab hold of to help you up. It could be the hand of a friend, a great new idea, or a belief system that lifts your spirits. In my life, whenever things are at their absolute gloomiest, a positive experience or event is almost always at hand.

It's not unusual for me to be a month behind on my mortgage and facing another month with no obvious means of income. That's usually the time when my car breaks down and threatens to write itself a check for whatever is left in my bank account. Yet sometimes money arrives when it's least expected, or someone shows up with an easy solution to a problem that had seemed hard to solve, or the car doesn't require an expensive repair job after all.

When things like that happen in the nick of time, I believe it is because life is constantly creating new and exciting opportunities. The Universe supplies. The Universe is a friendly and creative place. Watermelon magic exists.

Are you letting old and negative imprints from your past influence the choices you make in your daily life? Are you living in the past today? Perhaps you are walking through life the way a robot moves through a laboratory—controlled by someone else's program. You've got to switch off the automatic pilot and begin growing through life as a vibrant, healthy, self-propelled human being. Your goal should be to *grow* through life, not *go* through life. When you do that, you will become aware of the many options you have with every decision you make.

I have a friend who was the founder and chairman of a billion-dollar-a-year company when the board fired him. He could have wallowed in how he had built the company from scratch and become a big wheel, only to be now regarded as a fifth wheel. But he didn't waste a second on the past. He got a yellow legal pad and began listing his options for the future. In very short order, his life was rolling along in a new direction and he was happier and more productive than ever.

If you take time to examine your past, you will see it exactly for what it is: your past. You're traveling in the present. You can make your own decisions about the kind of person you are now. The you of your past can travel with the you of your present only at your invitation. Cancel the invitation. You will be doing yourself a big favor.

I'm not going to tell you that I was happy as each growth experience occurred. Like all of us, oftentimes I went kicking and screaming. However, as time passed, I worked on finding at least one positive element in each experience, and the more I focused on the positive, the clearer the lesson and the opportunity became. It's called *process*. You cannot change your past, but you can accept it, learn from it, use it to make your future different, and move on with your life. The quicker you can process it, the happier and more magical and peaceful your life becomes. The choice is yours.

It's amazing, but when I look back at pictures of the old me, under the spell of my old ways, I can't believe it's me. When I look at that guy, I see a stern young man who took himself all too seriously and tried to control people around him. There's no hint of the positive, happy-go-lucky Wally I am today. That guy wasn't the real me. He was an impostor. That guy could never manage a real smile. Smiling wasn't cool. Today, you don't have to say "Cheese" to get me to smile, but you could say "Watermelon"!

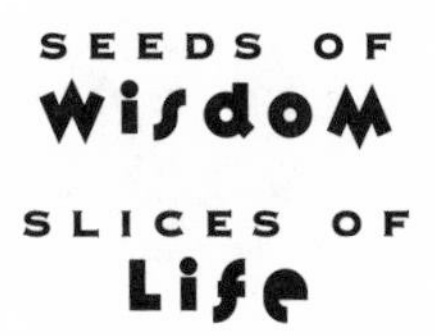

NO MATTER HOW MANY ANCHORS YOU'VE WRAPPED AROUND YOU, YOU'VE GOT TO BREAK FREE OF THEM IF YOU ARE TO MOVE ON. THE BEST WAY TO MOVE AHEAD IS ON A SPIRITUAL FOUNDATION. EVERYTHING ELSE IS TEMPORARY.

"THOSE WHO CANNOT REMEMBER THE PAST ARE CONDEMNED TO RELIVE IT."

George Santayana, *Life of Reason*

"IT IS THE UNQUESTIONING ACCEPTANCE OF THE ALREADY EXISTING THAT KEEPS PEOPLE FROM BEING CREATIVE."

Unknown

My experiences have shown me that life truly is a journey, and the less baggage we carry the easier the ride.

Wally Amos

Accepting Yourself

O Beloved Pan, and all ye other gods of this place, grant me to become beautiful in the inner man.

Socrates

Adults invariably coo at babies and say, "Oh, what a cute baby!" But if truth be told, criteria for cuteness in babies seems to be nonexistent. Like kittens and chicks and other miniature and helpless creatures, human babies are always considered cute. But there comes a point—could it be as early as four or five years old?—when adults and peers alike begin to weed out those who, in their opinion, are the beauties from those who, again in their opinion, are the beasts. Children become particularly adept and cruel at this, although you don't have to be a genius to guess where they learn it.

Can you remember the first time someone else ruled on how you looked—handsome, beautiful, plain, or ugly, or perhaps skinny, shapely, fat, short, or tall—as if it were as true as the boiling point of water? When, if ever, does an individual who has been pigeonholed as unattractive have the right of appeal with reference to the appraiser's criteria? Who empowered these self-appointed arbiters of beauty to pass judgment on anyone other than themselves?

Alas, it has probably always been that way. Even in ancient times, Aristotle remarked that personal beauty was a better recommendation than any letter of reference. If it were but a small percentage of individuals who judged their fellow humans by their cover rather than by content, perhaps we could do something about them. Martin Luther King Jr. also longed for the day when men and women would be judged not by the color of their skin but by their content. But Americans as a people, as much or more than others, seem to be hung-up on how people look. The dream merchants of Hollywood and the envy mongers of Madison Avenue have made us that way. For a century, they have been creating images that have become national, if not international, standards of beauty among those willing to buy into the illusion. According to *People* magazine, almost all of the World's Most Beautiful People are American film and television stars.

Unseen directors, image makers, and investors have engineered these false ideals and foisted them on others via idols such as movie stars and fashion models who, after a modicum of overexposure, become known as supermodels. Even our politicians cannot escape the curse of how they look. We insist that our presidents look "presidential." Candidates who aspire to lead the free world must have image consultants.

I've known some of the Beautiful People who achieved celebrity-envy status. Many made it on talent and character; others made it on looks and hype as much as anything else. That's fine with me, but some of us would rather be known for who we are, not how we look. Imagine for a minute how many talented, intelligent, and worthy people are ignored because they don't look like Beautiful People. When I was a personal manager, I sent my clients on casting interviews called "cattle calls" that had nothing to do with their talent or ability. It was demeaning and demoralizing for the actors and actresses when it turned out that the only criterion for landing the role was a certain inexplicable look the director had in mind.

Long ago, the makers of things realized that the things they made would sell better if they looked better. Of this need to improve the image of the product, not the quality, were born the industries of advertising, packaging, and marketing. Today, untold billions of dollars are spent each year on packaging products and people. In many cases, the packaging costs many times more than the product. Makers of laundry detergent put their powders into bright orange boxes to convey the image that the product is vigorous. The same powder could be packed in blue boxes to make it seem gentle. Millions of dollars are spent on research to determine which color will cause us to respond in a certain way. Aggressive claims are made in big letters and graphics that grab the eye. With so many bright boxes and slogans competing for attention, who would buy soap powder in a see-through box?

People are more complex than soap powders. Their qualities—good and bad—are hidden, although their faces, skin, and body shapes are not. We can't help but see their outsides first and begin to judge by what we see. How do we stop ourselves from making these assumptions and judgments based on looks—a decision as unfair as judging books by their covers?

In February 1995, *Newsweek* magazine published an extraordinary cover story called "What Color Is Black?" that questioned what Americans know and think they know about race. Senior writer Tom Morgenthau observed that Americans are preoccupied about the differences that divide black and white. The truth for those who will hear it is that the differences are no deeper than the skin color that has been an issue between and among the races for centuries. And the skin colors are so varied that color itself is no longer a question of black or white. In response to the question he posed, "What color is black?" Morgenthau answered: "It is every conceivable shade and hue from tan to ebony—and suddenly a matter of ideology and identity as much as pigmentation."

Scientists are finding that the observable differences between humans are virtually indefinable, while biologically we are essentially the same. "The bottom line, to most scientists," Morgenthau concluded, "is that race is a mere 'social construct,' a gamy mixture of prejudice, superstition and myth."

On one level, Americans are defining themselves into more groups than ever before. According to *Newsweek*, there are nearly three hundred races and ethnic groups. Hispanics have seventy categories of their own, and Native Americans have six hundred.

And then there's the Rainbow Generation of Americans who are neither black nor white nor Asian nor Indian nor any other established race, for they are offspring of two individuals of different races. The U.S. Census Bureau has buried its bureaucratic head in the sand by failing to recognize hundreds of thousands of citizens of mixed race in a category of their own, thereby requiring them to declare themselves as being of one race or the other. How can they be one or the other when they are both?

Happily, diversity is in these days. More and more institutions in the United States from the White House on down are trying to fashion their personnel rosters to look like America. While equal opportunity should mean ending discrimination against qualified individuals because of how they look or where they come from or what they believe, diversity can go too far if it means qualified people are denied the place they deserve so that someone who happens to be the Flavor of the Month can be promoted merely to be put on display.

When we look past the color of other people's skin, we're more likely to see that they are a lot like us.

Poets and artists have always been inspired by what they perceive as beauty, which is as it should be, if beauty is not equated with looks. Mark Twain said that the most beautiful thing he ever saw was a soap bubble. Sculptor Henry Moore said that to his eye a hippopotamus was far more beautiful than a swan.

Physical beauty, however it is defined, lies in the eye of the beholder. What turns people on in parts of Asia or Africa is very different from the ideal admired on Madison Avenue or in Madison, Wisconsin. Bo Derek was a ten in her director–husband John Derek's eyes, but not every judge at the Olympics sees things the same way.

Furthermore, attributes that are considered appealing today may be out of style tomorrow. One doesn't have to go back too far to find different ideals of beauty in our own culture. A century ago, Americans were clamoring to be plump. A patent medicine of the 1890s used the slogan "Makes Children and Adults As Fat As Pigs." If that company were around today, it would be selling the same tonic as a slimming preparation.

Popular looks are here today and changed tomorrow. Years after Twiggy's modeling career ended, the waif look came back with Kate Moss. Where was it in between those paragons of petite? What was wrong with the shape and color of Michael Jackson's nose before he copied Diana Ross's? What do pygmies think of Arnold Schwarzenegger? How sexy is a Marlboro Man if he is dying of cancer? Is it progress when women who berated Hugh Hefner for making young women into playmate sex objects with staples in their navels now read magazines featuring men in the same sort of poses?

People talk a lot about beauty when they are really talking about looks. A quipster posed the question "If beauty is skin-deep, why is lingerie so popular?" To my mind, the phrase "Beauty is only skin-deep" makes a lot of sense when restated this way: "Looks are only skin-deep." That's because beauty lies within, not atop the skin. Powders, creams, and all the plastic on the cosmetic surgeon's palette can't enhance it. Honesty, integrity, talent, dedication, and concern for humankind can't be grafted onto the human form. The danger of living in a society that reveres beauty and youth to the nth degree is that people judge others on their ornamental rather than inherent value. I like what actress Ashley Judd said when she was trying to understand Marilyn Monroe: "To me, beauty is a complicated issue; it's a prism through which a lot of colors are radiated. The most important colors to me are things like inner peace and understanding, and those are the things Marilyn lacked."

Coco Chanel, who knew a thing or two about beauty, once remarked that elegance doesn't come from putting on a pretty dress. And, she observed, "Nothing is ugly, so long as it is alive."

Avoid the trap of expecting to be treated a certain way because of what you appear to be. Expect the treatment you merit for being who you really are.

As a youngster growing up in segregated Florida, I never thought my skinny brown frame measured up to the other kids. I carried this low self-esteem with me to New York City, and my friend Walter Carter and I would lift weights so we wouldn't be taken advantage of like the underdogs in the Charles Atlas ads who got sand kicked in their faces. It has taken me years of inner work to finally realize I am the best-looking Wally Amos that ever lived, and that's good enough.

We are the only species that compares ourselves with each other. It doesn't happen in the animal world, nor in the world of fruits and vegetables. By and large we do it because of conditioning begun at an early age. I heard a six-year-old comment that jeans made her look fat. That was not her speaking, it was one of her parents.

Each of us is unique and special. No two sets of fingerprints are the same. Although twins appear alike, they too are different. Out of all the billions of people since the beginning of time, there will never be another you. So enjoy and appreciate your uniqueness. You are a priceless collector's item.

THINK OF A PERSON'S GOODNESS AS A WICK THAT WILL BURN TRUE NO MATTER WHAT SHAPE OR COLOR THE CANDLE AROUND IT TAKES.

"SUCCESS RESTS WITH HAVING THE COURAGE AND ENDURANCE AND ABOVE ALL THE WILL TO BECOME THE PERSON YOU ARE, HOWEVER PECULIAR THAT MAY BE. THEN YOU WILL BE ABLE TO SAY, 'I HAVE FOUND MY HERO AND HE IS ME.'"

Dr. George Sheehan

YOU ARE AN INDIVIDUALIZED EXPRESSION OF GOD.

"IT IS NOT WHAT I CALL YOU, IT'S WHAT YOU ANSWER TO: BUT IF YOU DON'T KNOW WHO YOU ARE, ANYONE CAN NAME YOU. IF ANYBODY CAN NAME YOU, YOU WILL ANSWER TO ANYTHING."

African proverb

YOU CANNOT BE A FAILURE WITHOUT YOUR OWN CONSENT.

"WE SUFFER NOT FROM OUR VICES AND OUR WEAKNESSES, BUT FROM OUR ILLUSIONS. WE ARE HAUNTED, NOT BY REALITY, BUT BY THOSE IMAGES WE HAVE PUT IN A PLACE OF REALITY."

Daniel Boorstin

"WE ARE TO OURSELVES JUST WHAT WE THINK WE ARE."

Quimby's law

Like people, watermelons come in many different varieties. They're round, fat, and striped. They're not the most attractive food on the outside, but they can be quite sweet and delightful on the inside. And both watermelons and people look the way the Creator intended for them to look. Why not accept our perfection?

Wally Amos

EMBRACING FAITH

"COME TO THE EDGE," HE SAID.
THEY SAID, "WE ARE AFRAID."
"COME TO THE EDGE," HE SAID.
THEY CAME. HE PUSHED THEM...
AND THEY FLEW.
Guillaume Apollinaire

How strong is your faith? Can a twenty-pound watermelon really grow from a tiny seed? You can count the seeds in a watermelon, but you can't count the watermelons in a seed.

A lot of people I know think they are too smart to believe in a Higher Power or to feel the need for spirituality in their lives. They look down their noses at people who go to church or who find joy in one's spiritual nature because they equate religious belief with ignorance and superstition. But their attitude is also based on a belief.

Albert Einstein was one of the greatest analytical thinkers the world has ever known, and he saw God quite clearly, though not in a test tube or an equation. In *The World As I See It,* Einstein noted that churches have always fought science. "On the other hand," Einstein wrote, "I maintain that cosmic religious feeling is the strongest and noblest incitement to scientific research."

As Einstein saw it, the more naïve believers hope to benefit from believing in God and fear punishment if they do not. Einstein said his own belief was based on a "sense of universal causation," a feeling that the way in which the Universe provides for our needs has nothing to do with the intellectual thinking and systematic acting of human beings. This spiritual feeling "takes the form of a rapturous amazement at the harmony of natural law," he said.

I'm not Einstein, but I am also struck by the magic of how everything works out in my favor when I don't struggle to impose my will but instead listen to the inner voice and allow my free will to create a positive reality. Like Einstein, I don't believe in an anthropomorphic God, a manlike deity who lives in heaven, listening to prayers, rewarding the good people who believe in and obey him, and punishing the evil people who do not. I do believe that just as there are laws of mathematics, science, and aerodynamics, there are laws that govern the Universe. When we allow those laws to work in our lives, we are in harmony. Faith is the starting point.

Some say that faith doesn't work for them, that believing in something doesn't make it real, and that praying for something doesn't make it happen. I know of a boy who was nine years old when his father suffered a heart attack. The little boy prayed and prayed for his father's recovery. When his dad died, the boy blamed God and never believed in God again. Nearly forty years later, he says that he is convinced there is no God and nothing to believe in. When asked what there is, he offers a line from the poet Dylan Thomas: "A force that through the green fuse shoots." He still cannot find a reason to believe.

It's easy to marvel at the beauty in a waterfall, a wilderness, a wild animal, a sunrise, a sunset, a strawberry, a watermelon, a newborn baby, a blossom, a bee, or a beach where we walk with our family. I believe there is more to the Universe than its outward aspects, lovely as they may be. I think there are certain aspects of the Universe that can't be seen or weighed or measured or explained. I am as certain that spiritual forces exist as the "green fuse" man is that a Higher Power doesn't. I know this because when I have needed help from spiritual forces, help has been there.

Only a year or so ago, it seemed I had lost or was about to lose nearly everything I had been working for. Events were turning my routine into chaos. My faith told me that if I kept going, kept searching for the answer, the turmoil could be calmed and I would come out OK. The thing is, the answer that comes isn't always the one you want or expect—but it turns out to be the answer you need. That's where acceptance comes in, and you're on your way, sailing off on a new course. It was my faith that helped me endure nineteen months of litigation over ownership of my name and likeness. The outcome wasn't exactly as I had envisioned; nonetheless, I accepted the outcome that was handed down and used it as a stepping-stone toward the next chapter in my life, certain that for every web begun, God sends the thread.

Writing this book is a great opportunity for me to revisit some of those moments in my life when I was helpless and did not have the answer—like the time in 1967 when I moved from New York City to Los Angeles with my wife and my two-month-old son, Shawn. I made the move to work with a client, only to be told by the client a month later that he no longer wanted me to represent him. I didn't panic or stress out. Instead, I remained calm. Soon after that, I received a call from a friend, John Levy, who managed Nancy Wilson, Joe Williams, and many other great artists, asking me to join his company.

Before I started Famous Amos, it looked like my career as a personal manager was falling apart. One client broke his ankle on the first night of a tour, putting his career on ice. Another client quit show business, a record company terminated another client's contract, and I gave yet another client his release. It looked like I was being forced out of show business. The reality was that I was being pushed *into* the cookie business. It is said we often go kicking and screaming to meet our good. Faith assures you that life is never really what it seems—it is always more.

As I write this chapter, the East Coast is experiencing its worst snowstorm in over seventy years. I've just spoken with a friend who said the storm made him realize he is not in control. He was scheduled to fly to Kansas but couldn't get out of his house, and even if he could have gotten out, all the roads and airports were closed. He had to wait patiently, having faith that the snow would stop, the roads would be cleared, and the airport would reopen. It brings into perspective the advice, "For peace of mind, give up being the General Manager of the Universe."

When obstacles mount, you must have faith that they can be overcome. You must somehow hold to the thought that everything is going to be all right, even though you don't know how, because that is beyond you. Somehow, throughout all my problems with the companies and the courts, I was able to maintain a sense of inner peace only because I trusted that everything was happening for a reason which I could not see or understand.

In matters of faith, there are many things you just accept. You don't have to understand them to accept them. I do a lot of traveling by plane, and I don't know how or why a 747 the size of a six-story building can fly through the air like a bird. Without understanding the laws of aerodynamics, I am willing to accept that jumbo jets can fly. These laws of nature apply whether passengers on the plane or people on the ground believe in them or not. I don't understand the laws of electricity either, but I know that when I plug something in or switch the lights on, electricity is all around me. I also know enough about electricity to know that if I stick my finger in the socket I'll get a shock. I believe that without fully understanding it.

Like the laws of aerodynamics, math, and science, there are laws of the Universe that control things. We don't see them or necessarily understand them, but they're still there functioning. I am not saying they control everything that happens to us; I am a firm believer in free will. I am saying there are universal laws that apply to our daily lives. These laws are available to us all. I have faith in them. I believe there is a Higher Force that keeps those heavier-than-air airplanes in the air and helps watermelons grow from a tiny seed.

Even those who refuse to picture a God in heaven or a Higher Power can see the evidence of faith in the genius and creativity that flow from great painters, sculptors, and builders like Michelangelo and composers like Handel who were inspired by faith.

Researchers have tried to prove the healing power of prayer. In one recent study, they showed that elderly heart patients were fourteen times less likely to die after surgery if they took comfort from religious faith and social interaction. In another, a doctor found that patients in a coronary care unit were far less likely to develop life-threatening complications if they took part in prayer sessions. And ninety-seven out of one hundred patients in an Alabama hospital said prayer was a big help in relieving their stress after surgery.

Whether it's prayer per se or just having the right outlook that cures, I believe that faith can move mountains to get past obstacles. Perhaps it's not believing that a physical mountain can be moved but taking the challenge that you see in your life as a mountain and reducing it to a molehill. Faith helps to change your perspective. The Universe is a positive place when you see it through the eyes of faith. Being positive on a regular basis seems to have both mental and physical benefits day after day.

On Christmas Eve last year, my neighbor and former landlady, Tinca, was riding her bike when she collided head-on with another bicycle. The crash knocked her off her bicycle, and despite the fact that she was wearing a helmet, she suffered a basal fracture to her skull. Her twin sister, Lucia, watched in horror as this happened. After the ambulance had taken Tinca to the hospital emergency room, my wife and I took Lucia to the hospital. Over the next several days I watched as Lucia experienced the impact of this horrible and unexpected occurrence.

At first she was full of anger. "What good was the helmet?" she fumed. "What if Tinca had not been wearing a helmet?" I thought. "I never ever want to see a bicycle again," she said. Of course we knew that the bicycle was not at fault. Lucia was focused on the negative aspects. She was not looking at what had really happened.

Setting aside negative emotions isn't easy, but when you look at situations with optimism and faith, you see things differently and focus your emotions on the more important things in life. By the next day, Lucia learned that Tinca had not been paralyzed. Although Tinca had not opened her eyes, she could speak. Lucia was seeing things differently as well. She had accepted what had happened, and she was regrouping and looking ahead. Tinca soon came home and showed improvement daily. While she was not expected to fully recover, there was every hope she would regain at least 95 percent of her abilities. During challenging times, when darkness looms, viewing things with a brighter, higher perspective is not easy. But it *is* possible. Everything is possible.

Focusing on the negative makes matters worse. Giving power to things increases them. Focusing on the positive can enhance your chances of moving ahead. You need to examine situations that confront you at different levels. It's a tree-and-forest thing. You've got to get high above the forest or far from it to appreciate the totality of it. Then you can focus on answers and solutions.

It takes objective thinking to work through challenging situations. Even if there is only an iota of positiveness, you must search to find it. It takes only a match to light up a room. If you sink into the negativity of a situation and start thinking of all the bad things that appear to be happening, the obstacles to your progress will only seem greater. If you focus on only the seeds in a watermelon, you miss the sweetness of the meat.

We all undergo gut-wrenching experiences that wind up changing our lives. Sometimes we never know why. An incident may seem so catastrophic or a situation so insurmountable when it happens, but then we look back at it sometime later and say, "Isn't it great how things turned out? Look at all the goodness that came from that experience!"

Emerson wrote, "The sun shines after every storm; there is a solution to every problem, and the soul's highest duty is to be of good cheer." Did you know that the literal translation of *worry* is "to strangle"? When we worry, we cut off our life supply of hope and magic. With worry there is no room for faith.

You've tried everything else, so starting today, give faith a chance. It takes faith to plant a little seed in the ground and be certain it will grow into a big, sweet, juicy watermelon.

How strong is your faith?

SERENDIPITY IS ANOTHER WORD FOR FAITH
AND CAN BE FOUND IN ALL OF LIFE, AT ALL TIMES,
AS PART OF NATURE'S LAW.

SERENDIPITY IS THE GIFT OF FINDING
VALUABLE OR AGREEABLE THINGS NOT
ACTUALLY SOUGHT FOR.

"FAITH IS STEPPING OUT ON NOTHING
AND LANDING ON SOMETHING."
Cornel West

"LIVING FAITH IS A ROCK WITH ROOTS."
P. K. Thomajan

At every turn in the road
during my journey,
my faith has confirmed
that life is a positive
experience.

WALLY AMOS

Changing jobs can be positive

TO BE PERFECT IS TO CHANGE OFTEN.

John Newman

Having a job has been one of the most important building blocks in my foundation. It has taught me to dedicate myself to doing a good job at whatever I do. It has fostered independence and created a sense of appreciation for what I earn. Yet as an insecure adolescent and a somewhat immature adult, I never had any career goals.

Like many people, I let the nebulous idea that I wanted to make lots of money lead me by the nose. Then, when I was making lots of money, I let the money dictate who I should be. It was only years later, when I knew who I was, that I came to understand that you have to enjoy what you do to be happy. I finally got the message that the reward is in the doing and that satisfaction comes from the process. Success is a journey, not a destination.

My journey has taken me on some very unusual paths. I have shined shoes, sold newspapers, delivered groceries, cooked in restaurants, attended secretarial school, been a member of the Air Force, and worked at

Saks Fifth Avenue, which led me to show business and then into the cookie business.

None of this was planned. I stumbled or slid from one thing to another. I'm tempted to look back and imagine that one experience moved me into another the way songs segue in a medley, but the changes were actually more abrupt—sometimes cliff-hangers. I quit Saks without having another job, and that took guts because I had a wife, a two-year-old, and another baby on the way. I had opportunities and I seized them, throwing off one thing and picking up another when it seemed right.

Some people stay at the same job for thirty, forty, or fifty years. It's easy to admire them if the work they do is fulfilling, rewarding, challenging, or somehow personally stimulating. But if they're clinging to a personally meaningless job for the sheer security of having it, or for fear of losing it, they're clogging the works so that new blood can't circulate past, and both they and the person they work for are losing out.

You can spend a lifetime in the same slot, without so much as a jiggle, waiting for the old gold watch and pension. Or you can roll yourself out of the slot you're in and find out what it's like somewhere else—across town, out on the Coast, or halfway around the world.

I've heard people say with pride that their parents taught them not to be quitters, as if quitters were kin to kidnappers. But I think there's a lot to be said for recognizing that there comes a time when terminating an interminable situation is better than digging into a dungheap and pretending it's a bed of roses. When Richard M. Nixon resigned the presidency in disgrace, he solemnly declared: "I have never been a quitter."

People talk about good timing. But good timing can only be seen in hindsight. When I started Famous Amos, the price of sugar was at an all-time high, margarine was high, and economic conditions were bad, so they said. I did not allow the naysayers to stop me. I went ahead and planted the seeds, and the results are now history.

Your future is waiting for you to act *now*. Whether you know it or not, what you're doing now is preparing you for what's next. Maybe you're not a home-run hitter, but you're swinging the bat in the on-deck circle and someone may be scouting your potential. What you're doing may not seem important, but how you do it may turn out to be. And what you do with what you've got—that's what people call experience.

Experience is important. If you don't give your best at what you're doing, you're not taking the necessary action to build a strong foundation. If I hadn't unloaded boxes well in my first weeks at Saks, they wouldn't have kept me on after the Christmas season. On the other hand, if I hadn't had the nerve to ask for a raise and the guts to leave when I was refused, I might still be there. And if I hadn't taken it upon myself to apply my supply-department experience from Saks to reorganizing the mailroom at the William Morris Agency, the agency might never have called on me to become its first black talent agent.

I was twenty-five when I joined the William Morris Agency in 1961 as a $50-a-week mailroom clerk. For the first time I sensed that a career lay ahead, and I was determined to make the most of it. I returned to night school on the G.I. Bill and practiced my typing during lunch breaks. Before long, I was a substitute secretary. Then I hit pay dirt as a talent agent.

Along the way, someone told me that what you give, you're gonna get. I gave it everything I had. I became obsessed with my work. I worked nights and weekends. By all accounts I had it made. There I was, booking rock-and-roll acts for a top agency, raking in big bucks, signing for meals and entertainment on an expense account, and neglecting my family. I was pretty much set for life with a pension plan and a profit-sharing plan. Man, I'd come a long way from the shoeshine box, but as it turned out, I still had a long way to go.

Before I found myself, I became addicted to the flashy, dress-to-kill, grab-a-buck business of entertainment. As a consequence of my twenty-five-hours-a-day Mr. Entertainment Agent lifestyle, I divorced my first wife, Maria, and married my second, Shirlee, who was a singer. I soon began to feel that the William Morris Agency wasn't treating me fairly, and my hand was itchy to try something else. In 1967, with a new wife and new baby, I quit the agency, quit New York City, and moved to California with nothing there to call my own.

The poet Kahlil Gibran, who said that work is love made visible, went on to say that "if you cannot work with love but only with distaste, it is better that you should leave your work and sit at the gate of the temple and take alms of those who work with joy."

To my mind, your work should be part of your joy. It should be something you want to do your best at. Even if you're not where you want to be on the ladder of success, it's best to know where you stand.

Too many people fear change. They cling to the familiar old shoe even if it cuts off circulation to their toes. When Bryant Gumbel announced he would leave the *Today Show* at the height of his success, he said it wasn't that he was totally fed up with the familiar routine that had made him famous. "But," Gumbel said, "fifteen years is a long time in one place, and the world's too exciting to enjoy from just one vantage point."

How are you going to walk or hope to run if you're chopping off your choices at the toes? And how many times have you heard people say that they won't make a change because they have job security?

To my mind, there is no such thing as job security. If you don't believe me, ask all the people who have worked for companies for years only to lose their jobs to downsizing. The illusion that you enjoy job security is not the same thing as being secure. True security rests on a spiritual foundation.

The most constant thing in life is change, from the level of every little cell in our bodies on up. Dr. Deepak Chopra reminds us that we can never step in the same river twice because the river is always changing and so are we. You never wake up in the same place twice. You are evolving. So are the persons and institutions around you. No company, system, or work situation is immune to change.

I don't recommend that people do what I did. What I'm saying is that your life is an evolutionary process and that you've got to open your eyes and your mind to all the change around you. What I'm asking is that you stop being a robot. Open your mind. Stretch out of your comfort zone. Don't be afraid to want more and be more. But be prepared to work for it, and in the end you will have a greater appreciation for what you get.

It is change that turns a seed into a watermelon. Stop resisting change. Embrace it and watch the seeds of your life grow.

THE WORLD IN WHICH WE ARE BORN IS NOT THE WORLD IN WHICH WE WILL DIE. CHANGE IS THE ONLY CONSTANT THING IN LIFE.

WE ARE HELD BACK ONLY BY OUR BELIEFS. IF YOU BELIEVE THAT WHERE YOU ARE AND WHAT YOU HAVE IS THE BEST YOU WILL EVER DO, THEN THAT'S WHERE YOU'LL STAY. IF YOU BELIEVE THAT LIFE CAN BE BETTER, THEN IT WILL BECOME BETTER.

SUCCESS DOES NOT COME TO YOU. YOU MUST GO TO IT. MY MOTHER ONCE TOLD ME, "YOU CAN'T GET ANYTHING IN A CLOSED FIST." YOU MUST BE OPEN-MINDED AND ACTIVELY INVOLVED IN CREATING YOUR SUCCESSES. MAKE YOUR OWN CHOICES RATHER THAN ALLOWING OTHERS TO CHOOSE FOR YOU.

"I DON'T BELIEVE IN CIRCUMSTANCES. THE PEOPLE WHO GET ON IN THE WORLD ARE THOSE WHO GET UP AND LOOK FOR THE CIRCUMSTANCES THEY WANT."

George Bernard Shaw

"LIFE IS WHAT HAPPENS TO YOU WHILE YOU'RE MAKING PLANS."

Spinoza

REMEMBER, SUCCESS IS A JOURNEY, NOT A DESTINATION. YOUR JOURNEY MIGHT TAKE YOU THROUGH MORE THAN ONE JOB OR CAREER.

we have been taught that our security is external in the form of a job or another person. the one thing i've learned from my job experiences is that through my thoughts and actions i control my world. if i think i will, then i will. the choice is always mine, and so it is with you. change is good!

WALLY AMOS

Gaining from Loss

WHEN ONE DOOR OF HAPPINESS CLOSES, ANOTHER ONE OPENS. OFTEN WE LOOK SO LONG AT THE CLOSED DOOR, THAT WE DO NOT SEE THE ONE THAT HAS BEEN OPENED.

Helen Keller

Our life is like our own private laboratory. We grow through life's experiences, no matter how good or bad they seem when they happen. The trick is to learn and gain strength from those experiences—especially from our losses. It's painful to lose someone you love, whether to a broken heart, a bitter divorce, or death, the ultimate destroyer of earthly relationships. Such a loss can rob you of your happiness and sense of security if you don't guard against that very thing. Losses may seem wholly negative at first, but I believe there is a positive way to look at everything.

Take divorce, for example. Like tuberculosis at the turn of the century, divorce is a stigma to some people, something that can only be discussed in hushed tones and an inference of shame. Not to me. I am the child of divorced parents, I divorced twice, and all three of my sons have divorced. You might say it runs in the family—or it ran through the family. I am not advocating divorce;

however, we're proof that there's life, and in many cases, far greater happiness after divorce.

Marriages are based on hope and promises. No one would willingly go to all the trouble of making elaborate arrangements and inviting all their friends and relatives to watch them walk down the aisle to take solemn vows if they thought the ceremony and celebration would end in divorce. While hope springs eternal and we promise to love and cherish one another till death, the fact is that the walk down the aisle sometimes leads to a dead end.

I was twelve years old when my mother and father divorced. They never were a loving couple. There were constant fights. Their fights were major events in my youth, like the preliminary and the featured events on a fight card. In those days, couples just sort of separated and went their separate ways without filing papers. One day, my mother just said that she and my father were not going to live together and that I was going to live with my Aunt Della in New York City. I said, that's fine, without thinking much of it. I never really felt any responsibility for their divorce. I could see it had nothing to do with me. As a result, I didn't feel deprived. My parents' divorce was a blessing because it helped make me who I am today.

If your parents have divorced, or if you've lost a parent in some other way, you will find other people who love you and care about you. They may not be a parent as defined by law, but if the love is there, the feeling of family is there. In my childhood, it was my Aunt Della who made the difference. She made me realize that I mattered. There were others along the way who made me feel whole as well. All they did was show that they cared.

Sometimes an organization provides "parental" support. Anton was a high-school dropout whose parents were divorced. He spent time with both parents and got along with them, but he felt lost and out of place. After he dropped out of school, for almost two months he did nothing but stay at home and watch television. His mother heard about Cities in Schools, a national dropout-prevention program, and was able to get him enrolled. Because Cities in Schools is based on love, support, and accountability, Anton's attitude eventually changed. He went on to graduate with honors and received a full four-year scholarship to college. As a leader in college, he started his own advertising business. Because he found love and support, Anton was able to turn his life around. He realized he was larger than his circumstances.

Years ago, you had to give a good reason to get divorced. Today, most divorces are "no-fault" proceedings where nobody has to claim responsibility for the collision or the damage. In my two failed marriages, I was at fault and I admit it. I was the one who fooled around, cheated, lied, and controlled my partner to get my way. I've had to face up to that and work to change the way I relate to people. It's made a big difference in my life and in my relationship with my wife, Christine.

The surgeon general hasn't posted warnings at the bridal registry or the bedroom, but a bad relationship can be detrimental to your health. Once you get to the point where you're saying, "I cannot stay in this relationship," prolonging the agony can be just *agony*. It can lead to anger, depression, and a lot worse.

There's no sense living as a prisoner of love if the prison is just a piece of paper. You can be a prisoner of love in a palace. Look at the horrible state that Prince Charles and Princess Diana got themselves into. Even the saintly but worldly Mother Teresa weighed in on Diana's crying need for divorce. "I know I should preach family love and unity," she said. But with Charles and Diana, she made an exception. "She is such a sad soul. It is good that it is over."

In both my first and second marriages, Maria and then Shirlee did everything they could to rescue the relationship. However, I had made my mind up that it couldn't be saved, so counseling couldn't help. Nothing could. In both instances, when the marriage broke up, my ex and I still had feelings for each other, and of course we were thinking about how our divorce would affect our children. Even the most callous person, wrapped up in himself or herself, must consider how the breakup will affect the children. Kids can be irreparably harmed by divorce.

When I look back on my decision to leave Maria and our two boys, it seems it was not so much a question of whether the choice was good or bad as it was one I had to make. Maria and I had the good sense and decency not to try to poison the children's minds against the other parent. We never used the children, ages four and two at the time, as pawns in our relationship.

I remarried and considered myself fortunate that my second wife, Shirlee, got along famously with my sons by Maria. Before long, and just about the time I was getting antsy and eager to move from New York to Los Angeles and make a big change in my life, along came my third son. Unfortunately, I wasn't any better the second time around at committing to my relationships, so my second marriage also ended in divorce.

Over time, the separation between my sons and I grew, and eventually we became distant. If there's a storybook ending here, it's that my sons and I have mended the major holes in our relationships. We're comfortable being together now and thoroughly enjoy each other's company. The four of us support each other in learning more about commitment.

Christine and I have been married seventeen years. I can't imagine getting divorced again. It's not that my marriage is 100 percent perfect, but Christine and

I have a great deal of harmony in our relationship, and we can talk about things. We have had separations, we've had counseling, and there were moments when our marriage could have ended in divorce. However, this time I joined in deciding that the marriage was worth saving. This time I joined my wife in a commitment to do just that. And we did. There was pain in making it work, but there would have been more pain in losing one another. Our happiness does not depend on our being married; we are in each other's life not by ownership, not strictly by law, but by choice. We plan to grow old together in a lasting friendship.

To keep a marriage or a friendship, you must work at keeping the lines of communication open. Ultimately you have to take responsibility for your actions in a relationship. You have to be responsive and supportive for a relationship to last.

It's easy to look at the past and to say things shouldn't have turned out that way. It's tempting to say, "I should have done this, I should have done that," but what's the point? I've heard that called "the tyranny of the *should*." You know you will never have the chance to redo things and keep on redoing them until you get them right, the way the Bill Murray character did in the movie *Groundhog Day*. At some point you must simply accept what has happened, and in accepting it, find the lessons that will make you a better person for learning them.

Eventually I saw that I had learned a lot about relationships from failing at them, and I learned a lot about being a father from being an all-too-distant one. Now I can see all the good that has come from my two divorces and from walking out on my three sons. I have grown a lot from those experiences.

Sometimes we allow ourselves to fly on automatic pilot. We don't recognize the need for a course adjustment. Then when it seems we are totally out of control, we consciously adjust our course and get back on track. After that, it's easy to look back and see where we were going wrong as well as how and why we changed course. Perhaps there were other paths to get us back on course, but we had to take the path we were led to. The important thing is that we accept what has brought us to where we are and steer a new course from that point forward.

I believe the most painful event in one's life is the loss of a loved one. I was on a combination book, cookie, and speaking tour in November 1994 when I got word that my mother was seriously ill. She had been ailing for many years, and in and out of hospitals since moving from Los Angeles to New York in August 1993. When I arrived at her bedside, she was slipping in and out of consciousness. I am not sure if she recognized me. Her lungs were filled with fluid and her heartbeat was irregular. The nurses had placed an oxygen mask over her mouth and nose to help her breathe. It was uncomfortable for her, so she kept taking it off. My son Michael said that it was just like her to be in control until the very end. The doctor examined her and advised that she probably would not make it through the night. We had decided to call the minister and the same mortician who had buried my grandmother, aunt, and uncle.

While I waited for them to arrive, I sat in a chair very close to my mom's bed. I actually wanted to get in bed with her, but I thought that would be too uncomfortable for her, so I sat in the chair and placed my head on her bed looking directly at her face. At that moment, I felt closer to my mother than ever before. Her skin was a beautiful golden brown and she looked very peaceful. As I lay with my head resting near hers, watching her breathe, I thought about how she had brought me into the world and now I was watching her leave the world. As I watched her breathing, it occurred to me that all of life is lived for this moment and that each breath could be our last, for we do not know what the future holds. I thought about how wonderful it was that in my mother's dying, I had gained a deeper perspective on living.

The minister and mortician arrived, and we all prayed with my son and my mother's sister, Lillie. During the whole experience I felt very peaceful and not saddened by what was taking place. My aunt and I sat down with the mortician to discuss how things would be handled in the event of my mother's death. I had never given any thought to burying my mother, but it all seemed very natural. Death is part of the continuum of life, and this was just another life experience. I was not feeling any sense of loss at all.

As it turned out, my mother did not die that night. Being at peace with myself and realizing there was nothing else I could do to help, the following morning I flew home to Hawaii.

Five days later, while preparing to do chores around the house, I got the call. My mother had taken her last breath on Saturday morning, November 26, 1994. Now, I see myself as a pretty spiritual guy. I've read books and thought a lot about death, and I suppose I had been subconsciously preparing for her death since she had been ill for so long, and she and I had long ago made peace with each other. But when I hung the phone up, my body started to go limp. I lost all desire to do anything. I started to weep, and a tremendous sadness came over me. Some people say you have to process grief. I think grief processes you. It took me quite some time to regain my composure.

I don't pretend that everything makes me happy. Her death saddened me, but not for long and not to the degree that I felt lost. I allowed my emotions to flow, and I rode it out. Sometimes I miss her a lot, and I always will, but I still don't feel a sense of loss. I guess that's because I never really thought I owned her. I also believe that life is eternal and that it's just the form that changes. God bless her current form wherever she may be.

I can't write about gaining from loss without thinking of my friend Max Cleland. There's a picture of Max on the wall in my office so that when I sit at my desk, he's smiling right at me. Max looks so handsome and happy and wholesome in that picture. You could never guess from looking at his joyous face what agonizing loss he's been through. If you read his book, *Strong at the Broken Places*, he'll tell you how he lost both his legs and his right arm while serving in Vietnam. There is a particularly harrowing part where he describes how hard he tried to walk using artificial legs attached to his stumps.

It proved too painful. He had to let go of that dream, let go of the idea he would walk, and accept the reality that he would be wheelchair-bound. That was years ago. Today, he is more active than most people with two legs. Max was the youngest person ever to be elected a state senator in Georgia, and he has so distinguished himself in public service that he seems destined to become a United States senator. When I told Max I was writing this chapter, "Gaining from Loss," he said that everyone has a chance for success and happiness no matter what they have lost.

"We all have obstacles to overcome," Max said. "As someone who has experienced a certain form of disability, you ultimately realize that all of us are disabled, one way or another, and the ultimate challenge is to do our best, regardless."

Max said he finds energy and meaning in his life by helping others. "We all have obstacles to overcome, though some challenges are greater than others. That's the nature of life itself. We all walk down a yellow brick road with a lot of obstacles and detours along the way."

Max says that when he faces the ups and downs, the mountaintops and the valleys of life, he takes them in stride. "I'm in my fifties," he said. "I just enjoy each day, and I do not let the past or future dominate."

The Hawaiian people have a special relationship with the land. They honor it and sing its praises in their songs. The American Indians also had a special feeling for the land. The idea of buying and selling land was strange to them. They equated it to buying and selling the sky, the freshness of the air, or the sparkle of the water. They believed that man belongs to the Earth, not the reverse.

It's time for us to return to the basics. No, not the three R's, but the basics of knowing that all things are connected and that we all are strands in the tapestry of life. Whatever we do to the tapestry, we do to ourselves.

In his book *Wherever You Go, There You Are*, Jon Kabat-Zinn wrote, "Giving does not exhaust your resources. At the deepest level, there is no giver, no gift, no receiver. Only the Universe rearranging itself."

The first time I read that was an "Aha!" moment for me. From it, I saw that there really are no losses in the Universe. We come into this world with nothing and we leave with nothing. So how is it that we get so hung up on owning things between the time we are born and the time we die? Ownership is an artificial concept that results from possessiveness, defensiveness, and greed. It exists only in its definition. The reality is that you can't own money or land. Even a fool understands you can't take it with you.

We often refer to our mates and our children as if we own them. We can't own anyone. In fact, we can't even own our own bodies. Owning something means having control over it, and I've yet to meet the person who has total control over his or her body. If you did, you wouldn't age and you would be able to make permanent changes to it. The reality is that we are all prisoners in a costume made of flesh that ages, decays, contracts diseases, and can easily be destroyed. We live in a borrowed vessel. Aging is a privilege.

Since you don't own your body, what truth is there beyond the body? When we can answer that question, we will find lasting peace. Then we will see that the Universe is truly rearranging itself and that, indeed, there are no losses.

"THE PAST IS BUT A BEGINNING OF A BEGINNING, AND ALL THAT IS AND HAS BEEN, IS BUT THE TWILIGHT OF THE DAWN."

H. G. Wells

IN THE CONTEXT OF LIFE THERE IS NO WINNING OR LOSING—ONLY THE PROCESS OF LIVING.

"IT CAME TO PASS. IT DID NOT COME TO STAY."

Eric Butterworth

"YOU CAN'T KILL LIFE."

Albert Roker

"THE SECRET TO HAPPINESS IS KEEPING YOUR MIND ON THE THINGS YOU WANT AND OFF THE THINGS YOU DON'T WANT."

Earl Nightingale

I think that life is a circle and that we are all holding hands as we stand in the circle. Whatever you give to the circle is returned to you tenfold plus. We spend too much time dwelling on what we are losing or what we don't have. Our focus needs to be only on giving. Giving is receiving.

WALLY AMOS

dreaming on, moving on

THE UNIVERSE ALWAYS SAYS YES.
Herman Afpink

**A THOUSAND-MILE JOURNEY
BEGINS WITH THE FIRST STEP.**
Confucius

Believing is essential to achieving your dreams, but it takes more than believing. At some point you must become actively involved in making your dreams come true. You need to plant the seed and nurture it so that your dreams will grow.

Are you dreaming of winning a $10 million sweepstakes prize from a company that sells magazine subscriptions? Perhaps you've been told you're one of five finalists in the nation tied to become one of the top winners of all time. It's funny how many other people in your town are about to break the same tie among the nation's top five winners! Never mind. With the extra one million dollars you're going to win because you ordered your magazines early, you'll be the envy of your neighbors when the television crew shows up at your door to announce you've won $11 million. As far as I know,

P. T. Barnum never sold magazines, but he knew that there is a sucker born every minute.

Why is it that so many people associate dreams with winning lotteries? Ask someone about their dreams, and likely as not, they'll tell you what they dream of owning. Their goals in life are material. I think we're conditioned to think materially. We're taught to believe that money and material things can change us and make our lives better. A lot of people think they'd be happy if they had a great car, or a big house, or fashionable goodies to stuff their houses with.

Though our dreams of tomorrow are important because they help us set our course, it is also important to feel a sense of accomplishment and fulfillment in the present moment. Toward this end, the lessons from yesterday show us how far we've come in our quest for self-fulfillment and happiness. Live each moment to the fullest. That's what makes dreams come true.

Years ago, I lived the Hollywood life of money, status symbols, and material things. Having them didn't make me happy. Unless you have more money than you'll ever need, in which case you wouldn't think about money, you'll probably never think you have enough. If you look to find meaning in owning things, you'll find that your things are never good enough and that the things end up owning you. You begin to compare your stuff with other people's stuff, and you decide your stuff isn't as good as their stuff, so you want better stuff. Then you need more money and a bigger house.

That's why materialism is acid soil for the roots of your happiness. The lessons of life are in unlearning all the false beliefs we've learned from advertising and other come-ons about the supposed satisfaction that comes from owning things. The only real way to find satisfaction in this material world of fads and fashions is to strip them away. Take off your clothes, your jewelry, and all your other magic charms. Stand there naked. Ask yourself, Am I enough without all that stuff? If the answer isn't yes, then begin immediately to find ways to create a new and improved you.

On a visit to Bentonville, Arkansas, to interest Wal-Mart in selling Uncle Noname cookies, I asked around trying to learn how much money Sam Walton had left when he died. I knew he was either the richest or one of the richest people in America, and I was curious just how much money that might be. I asked several people the question, "How much money did Sam Walton leave when he died?" One person had the correct answer: "All of it." You arrive with nothing and you leave with nothing. That's the bottom line.

John Lennon, the eccentric genius Beatle, had all the fame and fortune one young man could dream of having when he stripped naked and began dreaming of peace. Even as a lean and hungry musician before the Beatles hit it big, Lennon must have been thinking beyond the material rewards life has to offer. On the new Beatles anthology, when the Fab Four are doing their cover version of Barret Strong's big hit, "Money," they're singing the part that goes, "Money don't get everything it's true / but what it don't get I can't use," and right there in the hook where they sang, "Now give me money, that's what I want," Lennon ad-libbed, "Yeah, I want to be free."

I'm sure Lennon, who became one of the wealthiest entertainers of his era, understood that money brings neither happiness nor freedom of its own accord. That's why he went beyond conventionality to discover the depth of his art and spirituality.

As a kid I never had a dream or a career goal. I was driven only by the desire to make a lot of money. All my decisions were based on the same criterion: Will I make money from this? I even kissed my Aunt Della's feet once to make two dollars. Thank God they were clean. It wasn't until my late thirties, when I began to lose my materialistic desires and do things because I enjoyed doing them, that my life became more meaningful.

I attended a talk where the speaker described the circle of comfort in which we live our daily lives. If you remain within its familiarity, you deny yourself adventure, challenge, new experience, and growth. In order to grow, we need to go beyond what we know and feel. We have to go beyond our own comfort and familiarity.

That's where artists and inventors go. That's the "What if" realm where all great creations come from. That's where Steven Spielberg had to go in order make movies unlike all the others that had come before. The artist has to ask "What if" and let his or her imagination flow. Accepting the images and ideas out there in the creativity beyond the circle of comfort is as challenging as accepting what you find in the past. It's a process that takes us farther forward.

We all have the capacity to dream creative, constructive dreams. We can step out of the comfort of knowing everything around us into the comfort of knowing that we can accomplish things on our own. We've got to choke down that involuntary defeatist response that's in us. It's the one that says, "I'm not good enough. I'll never make anything of myself. That creative-energy stuff is OK for Steven Spielberg, but I'll never create anything that's any good." I felt like that when I started out in the career world, but I got over it when I realized I could come up with innovative ways to do whatever I was doing, whether it was a menial task or a mental task.

When I had the idea for my first book, *The Famous Amos Story: The Face That Launched a Thousand Chips,* I had never written a book. I didn't think I could. So I asked my friend Marcus Bach, who had written over twenty books, to help with it. For months I pleaded with Marcus because I just knew I wasn't up to the job. Finally,

Marcus said, "Wally, I really want to help you, but I'm just too busy. You can do it. Just write like you talk." Those words of encouragement got me started, and this is my fourth book.

If I can be creative, you can be creative. Who knows? You might have more talent than you think you do. Get a bigger-than-life dream and start chipping away at it. What's that? You say you'll never have a bigger-than-life dream? Neither did Spielberg when he started out. It starts by believing in yourself and relying on your God-given gifts of brains, judgment, and soul. Everything starts with an idea, and if you couldn't do it, you would never have gotten the idea.

Dreaming about winning a sweepstakes is the opposite of becoming self-reliant. If you're waiting for Ed McMahon or one of the other subscription shills to show up at your place with balloons, you probably aren't focused on getting yourself going. Ralph Waldo Emerson had these thoughts on self-reliance:

> There is a time in every man's education when he arrives at the conviction that envy is ignorance; that imitation is suicide; that he must take himself for better, for worse, as his portion; that though the wide universe is full of good, no kernel of nourishing corn can come to him but through his toil bestowed on that plot of ground which is given him to till. The

power which resides in him is new in nature and
none but he knows what he can do, nor does he
know until he has tried.

The problem is, if people think somebody else is going to do their work for them, they don't do it for themselves. It's easy for them to say, Hey, starting out is hard. Who issued the guarantee that life would be easy? The issue should never be whether a task is hard or easy. The only question I ask when approaching something is simply, "Is it possible?" I get a yes each time because all things are possible.

The Indian philosopher J. Krishnamurti observed, "The mind is not tranquil as long as it is traveling in order to arrive." When I think of a dream, I don't think of the prize at the end. I think of the journey toward the prize. Sometimes the destination is not as satisfying as the journey.

What I find magical is planning, creating, building, involving friends, and unifying talented people for a common goal. I am also motivated by improving on my previous successes. I find satisfaction in overcoming obstacles, finding paths that take me where I want to go, and having the experience of getting there in spite of it all. It's like the satisfaction you get when you look at your backyard after clearing the weeds. When you take out the weedwhacker and look at all those weeds, you think you'll never get them cut. But you cut the first weed and keep on going, and in a few hours you're finished. Confucius was right: The first step is the most important.

I also understand and accept that my dreams might not come to pass. I'm not foolish enough to think that just because I believe in myself or believe in my dream it will automatically happen. However, I will do everything in my power to make it happen. If it doesn't happen, I will not die or fall apart. I will not become discouraged. I will simply wait for another idea to come along. Then I'll pursue that dream with the same gusto and energy and enthusiasm I had for the last one.

So, how big should your dream be? Only you can make that decision. It could be gigantic or small. I can tell you this: The Universe is infinite. If you went to the ocean for water and only had a thimble, you could only bring back a thimbleful of water. If you took a ten-gallon bucket, you could fill that up. Dreaming is the same. The Universe will fill any size dream you give it.

Remember, it has to come from within you. Life is an inside job. Don't count on the Publishers Clearing House to deliver your dream to your door. If you have a giant craving for a large slice of juicy watermelon, you can't sit at home and dream it into the house. You have to get out of the house and go to the store to purchase it. Life is the same way. You must actively pursue your dreams to realize them. Dream on!

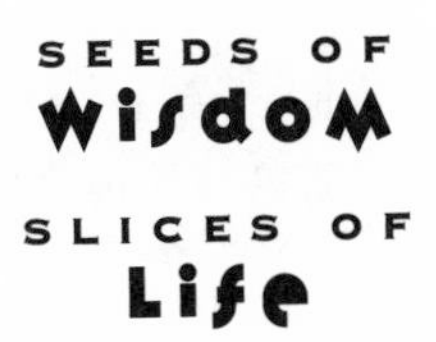

"DO NOT GO WHERE THE PATH MAY LEAD,
BUT GO INSTEAD WHERE THERE IS NO PATH
AND LEAVE A TRAIL."
Unknown

EACH NO GETS YOU CLOSER TO A YES.

EVERY PROBLEM IN YOUR WORLD
HAS THE POTENTIAL TO PROPEL YOU TO
YOUR WILDEST DREAMS.

"NOT HOW MUCH TALENT HAVE I,
BUT HOW MUCH WILL TO USE THE TALENT
THAT I HAVE, IS THE MAIN QUESTION."
W. C. Gannett

"OTHER PEOPLE CAN'T MAKE YOU SEE WITH
THEIR EYES. AT BEST THEY CAN ENCOURAGE
YOU TO USE YOUR OWN."
Aldous Huxley

dreaming big dreams is god's way of helping you do the impossible. following through on your dreams helps strengthen your belief in a power greater than yourself because you know you couldn't possibly perform such feats alone.

WALLY AMOS

HAVING FUN

MAKE A JOYFUL NOISE....
Psalms 100:1

Are you having as much fun as you can handle? Are you doing things because you enjoy them rather than because you feel you have to? Are you ready to live by the phrase "If it isn't fun, it isn't worth doing?" If you are, then read on.

The Old Testament says that man should eat bread by the sweat of his brow. The New Testament says that the man who doesn't want to work doesn't deserve to eat. More than a century after the Puritans imported the all-work, no-fun work ethic onto this continent, the acid wit of H. L. Mencken retaliated by observing that great artists are never Puritans. But the Puritans aren't the only people who frown at frolic.

Just about every organization from the Busy Bee Preschool on up the line of socialization tries to instill in us the value of hard work. Booker T. Washington advised in 1902 that no race can prosper until it learns there is as much dignity in tilling a field as there is in writing a poem. In *Up from Slavery,* he said that the only things worth having are those which come as a result of hard work.

Why are we working so hard? What is it about work that makes it so addictive? Although there is good reason to emphasize the dignity of labor today just as there was at the turn of the century, there is also a lot to be said for having fun and exercising our constitutional right to the pursuit of happiness. Henry David Thoreau, who sought peace of mind at Walden Pond in the last century, found great satisfaction in driving a nail home and clinching it properly. At the same time, however, he observed that "those who work too much don't work too hard."

I prefer to get things done as quickly and completely as possible to make time for fun things instead of dragging something out in order to fulfill someone else's idea of what being busy looks like. Some people will tell you that one excuse is as good as another for having fun. I say you don't need an excuse. I believe life is meant to be a fun experience. It's not as if you can't touch chocolate-chip cookie dough because it is destined to become cookies. You can help yourself to fun at any time.

Having fun in life is not an option, it's mandatory. If you're stuck in a job you don't enjoy, I'll bet there's a better job for you. For many reasons, years ago I had burned out on being an agent at the William Morris Agency. I was making more money than I had ever made in my life. I had status working for the largest and most prestigious theatrical agency at the time. I was respected and got to hobnob with the stars of show biz. I had everything but fun. The fun had drained out of me. I dreaded my work so much, I would walk forty-five blocks to the office to stall the start of my day. Finally after months of pain and agony, I resigned. It felt as if a mountain had been removed from my shoulders. I felt like a new man. My life did not fall apart. I went on to bigger, better, and more fun things. I never looked back.

For a while after I lost my financial stake in Famous Amos, the new owners retained me as a spokes-person. It was a cushy job. I established my schedule and what I would do, but it didn't sit right with me. I did not like the people who had bought the company, and the fun had left the cookie. On March 1, 1989, I walked away from a contract worth $225,000 a year that had three years left on it.

Your job is not your security. If you can't find enjoyment and fun in what you're doing, what's the sense of doing it? If you don't enjoy how you make your money, find another way. The reward is in the doing, not the paycheck at the end of the week, month, or year. Life is too short to be stuck in a job you hate with people you don't like.

In the household where I grew up, work was never seen as fun. My mother was a domestic worker who never saw any fun in cleaning someone else's house, even though she was very thorough and much in demand. My father was a laborer at the local gas plant whose work was dirty, but somehow whenever I visited him he never seemed to work hard. Anyway, I was always taught that work was more virtuous than fun.

It's widely held that work is loaded with positive attributes, while fun is usually portrayed as wasteful or foolish or sinful. We are led to believe that having fun will have its price to pay. As a kid I was told that dancing is a sin. The playwright Alexander Woollcott quipped that all the things he liked to do were either illegal, immoral, or fattening. People still feel guilty about having fun. But more and more we are beginning to hear, even from our industrious workaholic friends in Japan, that too much hard work is bad for your health.

Lots of people I know have it all planned out. They're going to work hard for thirty years, save all their money, and then retire and have fun. I heard about a jeweler who worked long hours, never taking a vacation, giving everything to his work so he could travel when he retired. Sure enough, he retired and took his long-awaited retirement trip to Hawaii, only to arrive at Honolulu Airport and die of a heart attack. Happiness is not a station you arrive at but a manner of traveling. You've got to live each day as if it were the last day of your life.

A vice president of personnel at a giant industrial corporation told me the average length of time they send retirement checks to their retirees is fifteen months.

We've all heard stories of people who made it to retirement, still full of vim and vigor, and then withered within weeks of getting that gold watch. One day you're active, all systems go, all faculties engaged, you've got a lot going for you, and then you retire. You don't have anything going, you don't have many interests outside of the work you no longer have, and you begin to atrophy. I think every day of work should be a day filled with things that excite you and stimulate your interest. You also need to supplement your work schedule with volunteer community involvement and plenty of time with family.

When you live every day planning for your future, you're really just planning to die. You miss out on all the wonderful things you could be doing every day. The truth is, the future is an illusion. It's a place that's impossible to get to. The only place you can ever be is here, in the now.

When my daughter Sarah was about three years old, we were landing in Los Angeles, and as she awoke, she asked, "Are we here yet?" Do you think she knew intuitively that "there" does not exist? I know we talk a lot about what we're going to do tomorrow, but as soon as we arrive in tomorrow, it becomes today. It's always today. If you're not living to the fullest today, you never will. If you're not having fun now because you're waiting for a better time or you think you need more something or someone, you're never going to have fun. If you are unhappy about something, change your mind. It's just a choice—your choice.

The worst thing in life is to reach a certain stage of your life, look back, and say, "I wish I'd done more. I wish I'd taken more trips when I had the chance. I wish I'd taken up a hobby when I was putting in all those health-robbing hours at the office." Life is not a video. You cannot press rewind, go back, and have another shot. How come you never hear anyone say, "I wish I had spent more time at the office?" By toiling for years longer than you'd like to, over work you don't even enjoy, you rob yourself of your life and the satisfaction that goes with it. Chances are, if all you do is work until it's time to retire, you're too tired or frustrated or sick to enjoy the money you've saved. You'll wind up giving it to the doctors, the undertakers, and the IRS. Wake up! Smell the watermelon. It's up to you to create our own "happy" and then take it with you everywhere you go. Find some fun activity that you've longed to do, and do it *now*!

Companies from Toronto to Tokyo and California to Kobe aren't as loyal to their employees as they used to be. They lay employees off, saying the bottom line is all that matters, not realizing that *people* are the bottom line. Big companies like IBM and AT&T, good ol' Big Blue and Ma Bell, let workers go by the tens of thousands when it suits them. Right there you have about 100,000 examples of why it's not wise to put off all your good times until retirement time.

Most of us think of our eyes as receivers of images. We tend to take situations as they appear to us, like a movie flickering on a giant screen before us. Oh look, we say. Life is full of hardships. I'm not making enough money. I'm miserable. Nobody loves me. Another way of seeing this is to regard our eyes as fountains pouring outward. We're the ones projecting the images we see onto life's screen.

Life is nothing until you say so. Each day is a brand-new canvas and you have another opportunity to paint the masterpiece of your choice. Paint happy, fun, and enthusiasm. Your thoughts create your reality. Don't give that responsibility to others. If you don't like what's happened in your life, change your thoughts. Abraham Lincoln gave us good advice when he said, "People are about as happy as they make up their minds to be."

Life is just one continuous movie with you as the star, the producer, the writer, and the editor. If you don't like what you're seeing, go to the projection booth of your life and change the picture that's on your screen. Yes, you are also the projector, and it's your responsibility to project the images you want to see through your own belief system. You can create the life you want. Don't let others into your projection booth—they may put a horror show on your screen.

You've heard it before: Every day is the first day of the rest of your life. Each day is also the greatest day of your eternal life, and every day is a day for having fun. The poet Robert Herrick said, "Gather ye rosebuds while ye may." I say you can't postpone breathing today so that you can breathe a few weeks from now or thirty years from now. No, you cannot accumulate breath for use later in life. The same is true for fun. You have to use it now. It's here to enjoy right now. Wouldn't it be great to enjoy every second you're breathing?

Remember when the multitalented Bobby McFerrin wrote and performed the song "Don't Worry, Be Happy"? That little ditty met with instant success because it delivered a message that people wanted to hear. It affirmed for them that they didn't have to worry round the clock, that they could take time out and have fun. Walter Hagen, the man who gave us the phrase "Be sure to smell the flowers," put it in this context: "Don't hurry. Don't worry. You're only here for a short visit." Elbert Hubbard, who specialized in one-liners called epigrams, put it this way: "Do not take life seriously—You will never get out of it alive." I coined my own phrase: "I'm not serious, but I'm responsible." You can be responsible and have fun. Serious people never have fun.

Laughter and enthusiasm are the wellsprings of life. We draw positive, nourishing energy from them. What's more, they're contagious. On many occasions

I've walked into a room laughing and playing my kazoo and have changed the energy in the entire room from gloom to happy in a heartbeat. When you serve up a batch of chocolate-chip cookies or cut open a big juicy watermelon, the energy inside a room can change in a minute from negative to positive, from ordinary to special.

If I spent all my time worrying about the money I owe or where my next paycheck was coming from to make my mortgage payment and pay other bills, I would be immobilized. Any time I spend worrying is time taken from focusing on solutions to my fiscal problems. By worrying over them I would become part of the problem, and I refuse to do that because I can only deal with problems effectively by removing myself from them and seeking answers and solutions. The problem is obvious: I have a negative cash-flow situation. The answer is simple: Make more money.

One of the best ways to give yourself a reality check or to reduce stress is to laugh at yourself. Laugh at all the dumb things you've done. Laugh at all the grand plans that blew up in your face. To laugh at oneself is the highest form of humility. Most of the laugh lines on my face come from laughing at situations I've gotten myself into. I can laugh at the big disappointments and the most inconsequential things that come to mind. I am constantly asking Christine where I put something, only to have her point it out to me in the most obvious place. I find myself laughing often when I am playing the role of parent with my daughter, Sarah. I consider the ability to laugh at anything—and myself in particular—an art and a blessing. A good laugh makes anything tolerable. A day without laughter is like a day without sunshine.

Years ago, to remind me that life is supposed to be fun, I started wearing loud and expressive socks. Putting on my socks was a reminder to have fun. I didn't care what others thought; those socks were solely for my benefit. Also, long ago I started living the title of Terry Cole-Whittaker's book *What You Think of Me Is None of My Business*. I soon discovered that my socks made others laugh and have fun too.

When I realized that my footwear could make people laugh, I asked Christine to paint a pair of tennis shoes for me. I started wearing them all the time, wherever I went, regardless of the occasion. When people greeted me, they would look at my feet before speaking to me, and soon I had a wardrobe of painted tennis shoes. Christine and I attended a state dinner at the White House during the Bush administration, and I wore my painted black tennis shoes, for formal wear, with my tuxedo. The president admired them and later sent Christine a pair of shoes to paint for Barbara.

On a subsequent visit to the White House for a Literacy gathering, I wore my regular painted white tennis shoes. Barbara noticed my shoes and commented how she knew I wanted her to wear hers, which I did. I told her it would be unbecoming for the first lady of our land to wear painted shoes in public. She asked if any reporters were present. Hearing that there were none, she asked her secretary to get her painted shoes from the bedroom. Wearing a stylish red dress with white polka dots and her ever-present pearls, she slipped into her white tennis shoes, painted with an assortment of flowers and a portrait of her dog Ranger on one foot and her dog Millie on the other. We took pictures and I went into the East Room to wait for her entry to address the group. I sat in the back of the room, and as she got about a third of the way down the aisle, I yelled out, "Look at those shoes!" The whole room broke out in laughter with Barbara taking the lead. She is a gracious lady who knows the value of laughter. Laughter knows no barriers.

The reality is that we all live hand-to-mouth and month-to-month because we never know what lies ahead. Sure, we have goals and long-range plans, but we never know when our next breath will be our last. It could happen at a moment's notice. My friend Bob Goodale, who is one of the happiest people I know, says he does not necessarily wish to die this moment, but if this should be his time to go, his bags are packed.

I am also reminded daily that there are no facts on the future. That's why it's best to make use of every breath we have. That's why we have to take some more time to eat and enjoy the watermelon. Even when we're engaged in the supposedly serious activities of life, we have to stop the treadmill, jump off, look back, and laugh at the way we are and the things we do when we're on it. I sincerely believe the one thing that has gotten me through all my challenges has been my ability to laugh and have fun. I can remember years ago saying to myself, "I am not going to have any more bummer days." I meant it, and I haven't. It was a conscious choice made by me.

Taking charge of your thoughts is a choice. Make that choice today! Life was meant to be a fun and fulfilling experience. Don't let yours be the exception. Start having fun today!

"JOY IS THE INFALLIBLE SIGN OF THE PRESENCE OF GOD."
Teilhard de Chardin

"AS I GET OLDER, I SEEM TO PLACE LESS IMPORTANCE ON MATERIAL THINGS. COME TO THINK OF IT, I PLACE LESS IMPORTANCE ON IMPORTANCE."
Tim Hansel, *You Gotta Keep Dancin'*

"MOST MEN PURSUE PLEASURE WITH SUCH RECKLESS HASTE THAT THEY HURRY PAST IT."
Soren Kierkegaard, *Either-Or*

"A MAN HATH NO BETTER THING UNDER THE SUN, THAN TO EAT, AND TO DRINK, AND TO BE MERRY."
Ecclesiastes 8:15

"I do not like work, even when another man does it."

Mark Twain

"Happiness is a habit—Cultivate it."

Elbert Hubbard, *Book of Epigrams*

Obituaries always list the year you were born and the year you died, separated by a dash, 1900–1996. When you were born or when you died is not nearly as important as what you did in between—what you put in your dash.

What have you put in your dash? The older I get, the more fun I want to put in my dash. If it's not fun, I won't do it.

Wally Amos

epilogue

When you think of it, there are some parallels between watermelons and humans. Here are a few I've come up with.

As the umbilical cord ushers a mother's blood filled with nutrients into her child, so the watermelon vine carries the nurturing life force of the earth into a tiny flower that becomes the heavenly object known as watermelon.

Vines alone are prickly, unappealing things. The same can be said for the thorny events in our lives that we would rather overlook than look over. The vine is the connection that watermelons have in common. Our connection is the vine of Spirit.

The big green leaves that spring from the vine protect the watermelons from the sun and wind. We are also protected during our early years, not by leaves, but by loving parents, relatives, or friends.

To the eye, a watermelon field is a sea of circular objects. From afar each emerald-green case looks identical to every other; yet up close each is as uniquely swirled as a fingerprint. From a distance, we too look identical, but when we get up close and personal we become aware of our unique, individual qualities. Watermelons come in all sizes, hues, and shapes. Still, they are all born of a vine, the way humankind, of different sizes, shapes, and hues, are all born of woman.

George Bernard Shaw wrote of being used for a purpose recognized as a mighty one and of being thoroughly used up when he died. We can take a cue from watermelon, for every part of the melon is used. My mother pickled the rind when I was a kid; you can drink the juice; the seeds can be toasted for snacks or used to grow more watermelons; and of course you can eat the meat, or as watermelon farmers say, the flesh, which is another connection. Watermelon not only satisfies, it's fun and it motivates.

All the actions and events in our lives are linked, as if on a vine. We cannot detach ourselves from the constant vine that binds us to our past and energizes our future. Just as all watermelons are not as sweet as we anticipate, all of our life situations will not rise to our expectations. Yet if we choose to, we can work for and attain the sweetness that surges through the vines of our lives.

Thanks for spending time with me. May all your days be as sweet as the sweetest piece of watermelon you will ever eat.

Have a sweet life!

Aloha,

Wally Amos

Wally Amos
aka Wallymelon

For information on literacy, contact

Literacy Volunteers of America
5795 Widewaters Parkway
Syracuse, NY 13214
(315) 445-8000

National Center for Family Literacy
Waterfront Plaza, Suite 200
325 W. Main Street
Louisville, KY 40202
(502) 584-1133

For information on dropout prevention, contact

Cities in Schools
1199 N. Fairfax Street, Suite 30
Alexandria, VA 22314
(703) 519-8999

For information on lectures by Wally Amos, contact

Penny Hunt
2605 Rippee Road
Tallahassee, FL 32303
(904) 514-3013

OTHER BOOKS FROM BEYOND WORDS PUBLISHING, INC.

The Woman's Book of Creativity

Author: C Diane Ealy, $12.95 softcover; $16.95 two audiotapes

Creativity works differently in women and men, and women are most creative when they tap into the process that is unique to their own nature—a holistic, "spiraling" approach. The book is a self-help manual, both inspirational and practical, for igniting female creative fire. Ealy encourages women to acknowledge their own creativity, often in achievements they take for granted. She also gives a wealth of suggestions and exercises to enable women to recognize their own creative power and to access it consistently and effectively. Ealy holds a doctorate in behavioral science and consults with individuals and corporations on creativity.

Nurturing Spirituality in Children

Author: Peggy D. Jenkins, $10.95 softcover

Children who develop a healthy balance of mind and spirit enter adulthood with higher self-esteem, better able to respond to life's challenges. This book offers scores of simple and thought-provoking lessons that parents can teach to their children in less than ten minutes at a time. Using items easily found around the house, each lesson provides a valuable message for children to take into their days and into their lives. The lessons are easy to prepare and understand, and each parent can alter the lessons to fit their own spiritual beliefs. The activities are adaptable for children from preschool to high school ages.

The Book of Goddesses

Author/illustrator: Kris Waldherr

Introduction: Linda Schierse Leonard, Ph.D., $17.95 hardcover

This beautifully illustrated book introduces readers of all ages to twenty-six goddesses and heroines from cultures around the world. In the descriptions of these archetypal women, the author weaves a picture of the beauty, individuality, and unique strength which are the birthright of every girl and woman. Beautiful to look at and inspiring to read, this book is a stunning gift for goddess-lovers of all ages.

Know Your Truth, Speak Your Truth, Live Your Truth

Author: Eileen R. Hannegan, $12.95 softcover

To be truly yourself, you need to have an authentic integration of the mental, emotional, physical, and spiritual truths of self. This book offers a simplified formula of the ancient truths that escort an individual into personal and spiritual wholeness. The three-part program assists individuals in discovering the truth of who they truly are and thereby in living a more authentic life.

You Can Have It All

Author: Arnold M. Patent, $16.95 hardcover

Joy, peace, abundance—these gifts of the Universe are available to each of us whenever we choose to play the real game of life: the game of mutual support. *You Can Have It All* is a guidebook that shows us how to move beyond our beliefs in struggle and shortage, open our hearts, and enjoy a life of true ecstasy. Arnold Patent first self-published *You Can Have It All* in 1984, and it became a classic with over 200,000 copies in print. This revised and expanded edition reflects his greater understanding of the principles and offers practical suggestions as well as simple exercises for improving the quality of our lives.

Home Sweeter Home: Creating a Haven of Simplicity and Spirit

Author: Jann Mitchell
Foreword: Jack Canfield, $12.95 softcover

We search the world for spirituality and peace—only to discover that happiness and satisfaction are not found "out there" in the world but right here in our houses and in our hearts. Award-winning journalist and author Jann Mitchell offers creative insights and suggestions for making our home life more nurturing, spiritual, and rewarding for ourselves, our families, and our friends.

Letters from the Light: An Afterlife Journal from the Self-Lighted World

Author: Elsa Barker; Editor: Kathy Hart, $12.95 hardcover

In the early part of this century, a woman begins a process of "automatic writing." It is as though someone takes over her hand and writes the document. Days later she finds out that the man has died thousands of miles away, and she is now serving as a conduit as he tells of life after death through her. His message: There is nothing to fear in death, and the life after this one is similar in many ways to the one we already know, even though we will be much more able to recognize our freedom. Readers of the book, originally published in 1914, invariably concur that the book removed from them the fear of dying.

Beyond Words Publishing, Inc.

Our corporate mission:

Inspire to Integrity

Our declared values:

We give to all of life as life has given us.

We honor all relationships.

Trust and stewardship are integral to fulfilling dreams.

Collaboration is essential to create miracles.

Creativity and aesthetics nourish the soul.

Unlimited thinking is fundamental.

Living your passion is vital.

Joy and humor open our hearts to growth.

It is important to remind ourselves of love.